**Dedicated to Maria and Frederick
and to the generations they inspired.**

"Weiß doch der Gärtner, wenn das Bäumchen grünt,
Daß Blüt' und Frucht die künft'gen Jahre zieren."

"But the Gardener knows, when the young tree's leaves first appear,
That flowers and fruit will grace the future years."

From *Faust, Part One: Prologue in Heaven*, Scene 3, lines 310-311
By Johann Wolfgang von Goethe
Free translation by Paul Bentel

Carol Rusche Bentel
Paul Bentel
Peter Bentel
John Morris Dixon

CORRELATIONS: LIFE + WORK
Bentel & Bentel Architects

CONTENTS

7   **FOREWORD**

8   **WHO WE ARE**
10   Family Houses
22   Firm and Family
34   Firm and Family: Design Philosophy
58   Firm and Family: The Next Generation

61   **WHAT WE DO**
63   St. Stephen the First Martyr Church
68   Gramercy Tavern
72   Bethpage Public Library
76   Cor Jesu Academy
81   Parish of the Holy Cross
84   Eleven Madison Park
88   Resource and Image Center, SVA
90   Charapani
94   Craft
98   The Modern
104   Miller Library, Waldorf School
107   Rouge Tomate
110   Red Rock Casino, VIP Suites
116   Axinn Library, Hofstra University
122   W Hotel, Market Restaurant, and Descent Bar
130   Le Bernardin

136	Apella and Riverpark	**216**	**WHO WE WERE**
144	Grand Hyatt Hotel	217	Firm and Family
149	Ground Café, Yale University	219	Maria Azzarone's Family
152	Hyatt Regency	219	Frederick Bentel's Family
160	Renwick Gallery	220	Meeting at MIT
162	Rouge Tomate Chelsea	220	Early Work in New York City
167	Club 432	220	Early Work, 1953–1960
170	41 Linskey Way	224	Variations on Modernist Themes, 1960–1970
173	Couch Academic Center, Webb Institute	231	Suburban Modernism and Community Architecture, 1970–1980
176	Palms Casino Resort	235	A New Formalism, 1980–1990
184	Hall Arts Hotel	236	Re-establishing the Progressive Ethic
192	Hudson Yards Grill		
197	Small Batch		
202	Hunter Restaurant		
208	601 Lexington Avenue Atrium	**238**	**ABOUT THE AUTHORS**
212	Oakland Park Design Guidelines	**239**	**ACKNOWLEDGMENTS**

FOREWORD

John Morris Dixon, FAIA

The founding of Bentel & Bentel by two architects, Dr. Frederick and Maria Bentel, joined by marriage was highly unusual in the 1950s—but not unique. The evolution of both firm and family in the decades since, however, has produced an integration of family life and design practice so rare that we know of no close parallels. The founding couple's two sons, Paul and Peter, along with Paul's wife Carol, joined the firm in the 1980s, worked with the senior Bentels for decades, then took on the lead roles in the practice. And today grandchildren of the founders are pursuing design studies that may well yield yet a third generation of principals for this firm.

There are other distinctive aspects of the Bentels' life that contribute to the solidarity of both firm and family. Two current generations of the family now occupy two houses Maria and Fred designed at the outset of their practice. And their design practice continues to take place in the same exceptional office the founders adapted from a suburban house. The work space has a multilevel, skylit volume with no partitions at all, facilitating interaction among partners and staff.

The closeness of the partners is reinforced by educational programs they have pursued, often overlapping in terms of distinguished schools they have attended. From the founding of the firm, its partners have also taught complementary design-related subjects. Intellectual and philosophical bonds among them are also reinforced by steady involvement in the arts, in teaching and research, and in professional organizations.

Practicing architecture with partners who are also relatives has lent the firm an unusual consistency in its design objectives and procedures. Yet these complex relationships have by no means led to design uniformity in their works. Instead, these architects have shared a commitment to fulfill each commission with a very particular design that best suits its specific demands and potentials.

Among the outcomes of this rare interweaving of experiences, lifestyles, and personal philosophies has been an impressive series of architectural works, including public buildings, educational environments, restaurants, and hotels—all notable for their thoughtful relationship to those they serve and the communities in which they stand. Reflecting on the integrated lives and accomplishments of the firm's partners over some six decades, this book is composed of three complementary narratives: Who We Are, What We Do, and Who We Were.

WHO WE ARE

We are a firm and a family. We are an architecture and interior design firm built on foundations laid by the preceding generation of firm and family and inspired by earlier eras of craft-makers and builders.

We are Paul and Peter Bentel (brothers) and Carol Rusche Bentel (wife of Paul), partners at Bentel & Bentel Architects. We have been trained at various institutions, some overlapping, and our common interests include the arts, the use of authentic materials, and the design of spaces that embody the inherent culture and activities of the place. We desire to create architecture that is transformative and inspires its users. We believe that the experience of our work allows the people who inhabit it a deeper understanding of the place.

In our opinion, the design process consummates in real things: urban areas, buildings, interiors, furniture, objects of daily use. Thus, we seek emotive power for our work principally in its physical attributes rather than through reference or allusion. We aspire to foster experiences that are more than sensually gratifying. A firsthand encounter with great design can capture the senses and ignite the imagination; such moments hold value for both the individual and society at large.

The most challenging aspect of architectural design is the transformation of an idea—a fragile and insubstantial notion about how a space should be formed, or an object constructed—into a thing. So much depends on the ability to translate ideas into physical form, to understand how a building or interior space can be made. Once a direction is determined—about materials, structure, aesthetic—the central challenge is allowing it to grow and change without excessive compromise.

Because we believe that great design presents the new and resists the conventional, we strive to do work that is singular and authentic.

We bring to this task broad experience and training in the arts, building crafts, architectural history, construction, engineering, and the physical and social sciences. Each of us also studied and practiced as a visual and performing artist (painting, printmaking, and sculpture; theater, dance, and choreography). We typically work with large drawings and full-scale models, using the proposed materials for each project with an eye to assessing both their effect and dramatic character. We consider collaborations with artists and craftspeople essential to this process. Our ultimate goal is to explore the possible in order to achieve exceptional craftsmanship and detail that engages people in unparalleled ways.

We cherish the role of the constructed environment as a stimulus to individual revelation, social interaction, and community identity. Though it can be challenging, our design work is not arcane. We pursue intelligent engagement with the people who use what we create. The power of our work may be attributed to the thoughtful and expressive structuring of appropriate parts into an absorbing whole. In the end, what we seek is unprecedented design that redefines rather than reproduces prevailing conventions.

CORRELATIONS: LIFE + WORK BENTEL & BENTEL ARCHITECTS

ORCHARD HOUSE

LATTINGTOWN, NEW YORK | 1959

Three generations of Bentels have flourished in Orchard House in Lattingtown, Long Island. Completed in 1959, it was designed by Bentel & Bentel founders Maria and Fred Bentel for Maria's parents, Louis and Teresa Azzarone. Situated on a historic estate, the Modernist residence hovers over a rectangle of apple orchard enclosed by granite walls. Carol and Paul Bentel are the current occupants of the house, which is also a gallery for artworks from all generations.

Many of the orchard's apple trees, more than a century old, still thrive on the Orchard House site. Curved vaults and concrete columns in rows that replicate the silhouette and layout of the trees pay homage to the setting.

WHO WE ARE FAMILY HOUSES

LEFT: Front of Orchard House and entry bridge ABOVE: Orchard House interior, with spoon sculpture *Sperm and Egg* by Michela Bentel, 2014 BELOW: Rear view of house from orchard FOLLOWING PAGES: Orchard House living room

CORRELATIONS: LIFE + WORK **BENTEL & BENTEL ARCHITECTS**

LINDEN HOUSE

LATTINGTOWN, NEW YORK | 1959

On a richly wooded site across the road from the Orchard House is the residence Maria and Fred created for themselves and their children, now the renovated residence of Peter Bentel. Its wings are laid out to weave among the numerous trees. The lower level of the right wing was designed to house the original Bentel office, accessible through its own public entrance.

This house originally formed a U-shaped space around a tall specimen linden tree, which unfortunately succumbed to storm winds in 2020 and has been replaced by a carefully chosen young white oak. The materials are consistent with the Orchard House: concrete structural frame with brick infill walls and areas of glass framing landscape views and vaulted roofs lending greater scale to main living spaces.

Today, second and third generation Bentel families occupy both the Orchard and Linden Houses. Distinctive design features such as reflective lacquered ceilings, various cuts of white oak, and brick walls punctured by individual glass blocks attest to the family's interest in material investigations over several decades.

RIGHT: Linden House front

WHO WE ARE   FAMILY HOUSES

CORRELATIONS: LIFE + WORK BENTEL & BENTEL ARCHITECTS

RIGHT: Linden House entry in glazed link
BELOW: Linden House, rear view
OPPOSITE: Linden House interiors

WHO WE ARE FAMILY HOUSES

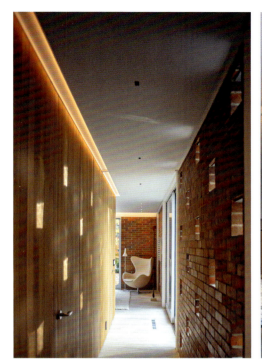
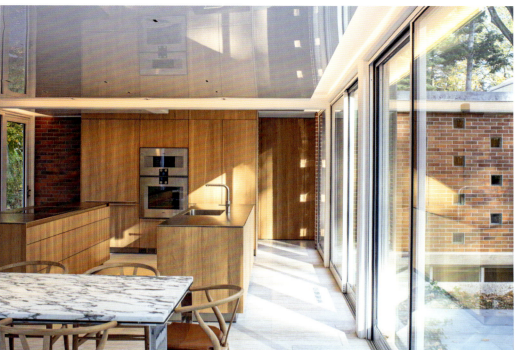

CORRELATIONS: LIFE + WORK   BENTEL & BENTEL ARCHITECTS

LUCCA HOUSES

LUCCA, ITALY | 1994

In 1990, the Bentel family acquired a half-ruined property in Lucca, Italy, within an olive grove and near marble quarries. Casa Grande, the larger of two structures on the site, rises across an open piazzetta from Casa Piccola. We renovated the houses and grounds over time, keeping the architectural spirit of the place on the exterior while creating a language of our own within. The culinary arts and the fine arts (particularly sculpting marble) are part of our everyday life in the tranquil Tuscan setting.

RIGHT: Night view of Casa Piccola from olive grove

WHO WE ARE   FAMILY HOUSES

CORRELATIONS: LIFE + WORK   BENTEL & BENTEL ARCHITECTS

THIS PAGE (CLOCKWISE FROM TOP LEFT): Renovated hay barn with sculpture studio addition at dusk; Writing loft above sculpture studio; Pool; Distant view of houses from olive grove
OPPOSITE (CLOCKWISE FROM TOP LEFT): Piazzetta with solar fountain, also used for evening dining; Casa Grande living room; Piazzetta with four cypresses between the two houses

20

WHO WE ARE   FAMILY HOUSES

CORRELATIONS: LIFE + WORK   BENTEL & BENTEL ARCHITECTS

FIRM AND FAMILY

The current partners of Bentel & Bentel work in a distinctive office: an old barn turned residence turned architect's studio in Locust Valley, Long Island. Original partners Maria and Fred modified the building in the 1970s, adding a large, open volume in the center of the structure. Multilevel platforms around this skylit space meet functional needs and at the same time sustain the firm's egalitarian spirit.

Our studio spaces, characterized by ample daylight and unusual vistas, encourage spontaneous design discussions. Scattered throughout the office are architectural models, full-scale mock-ups, hand sketches, veneer flitches, colorful prints, carving tools, chair prototypes, glass and millwork samples, carpet swatches, and stone specimens.

Our library, assembled by the two generations of Bentel & Bentel partners, feeds our interests in architectural history and theory. The most extensive sections cover the 1930s, Italian Modernism, American architecture between the wars, and the English Arts and Crafts movement. Sliding ladders allow access to the upper shelves and to two loft spaces. The library can be used as an event space for groups or a quiet respite for individuals. In our principal meeting room nearby, sculptures by firm partners are juxtaposed with the spiral stair leading to a third loft.

RIGHT: Firm library
FOLLOWING PAGES (LEFT TO RIGHT): Spiral stair in conference room to office loft and sculptures, 1980, by Paul Bentel; Studio workspace
PAGES 26-27: Paul Bentel, Peter Bentel, and Carol Rusche Bentel

WHO WE ARE   FIRM AND FAMILY

CORRELATIONS: LIFE + WORK   BENTEL & BENTEL ARCHITECTS

WHO WE ARE FIRM AND FAMILY

CORRELATIONS: LIFE + WORK   BENTEL & BENTEL ARCHITECTS

PAUL BENTEL, FAIA

It is not easy to convey how deeply immersed we were as kids in the culture of material transformation. Our family consisted of artisans, builders, engineers, and architects pursuing livelihoods invested in making things. Our "immersion" was literal as well as metaphorical. As with my siblings and cousins, I grew up in a house that was made by our family. Its design idiosyncrasies, testaments to the collaboration between young architects and seasoned builders working in reinforced concrete, were mirrored on its interior in modern art and accessories by, among others, Jose Luis Sert (our neighbor for a time), George Nelson, Carl Auböck, and Costantino Nivola. As children, we entertained ourselves in our parents' library, which held a memorable collection of books displaying the work of the likes of Le Corbusier and Frank Lloyd Wright. I recognize now to what degree *Townscape* by Gordon Cullen and *The Design of Cities* by Edmund Bacon inspired my interest in drawing buildings and visualizing environments.

Formative personal engagement with the culture of making things accompanied this ad hoc immersive "learning." During our parents' frequent business trips, we spent days with our paternal grandparents, Maria and Karl, and Uncle Charles. Karl, a German cabinetmaker, and "Charlie," an electrical engineer, taught us to use the machinery and materials in their shop while Maria taught us to make the cakes, prepare the meats, and preserve the vegetables she knew as a girl raised on a farm in Germany. We made things with them and learned for ourselves the art of transforming raw materials into objects fashioned after our own designs.

Houses occupy a significant place in my recollections of childhood. In the 1960s, our parents built a second house adjacent to a garnet quarry in the Adirondack Mountains. We spent weekends camped in the unfinished structure as it took form on a site where we had formerly camped in a tent. That place in the woods adjacent to the massive pile of rock overburden extracted years before from the quarry projected its own visual and formal vocabulary. The three-dimensional palette formed out of fluid tree forms set against the ragged quarry walls still inspires my sculpture.

Sculpture gave me a tangible outlet for thoughts and ambitions forged out of this upbringing. At first, the objects I made were simple exercises in clay, plaster, stone, and metal. Later, they held a meaning greater than the outcome of a process. In high school, I studied sculpture under the painter, sculptor, and set designer Cabot Lyford and worked in stone, welded steel, and cast metal. At Harvard College, I continued in studio art, working primarily with Dimitri Hadzi. There I focused on figural plaster pieces, large three-dimensional

WHO WE ARE   FIRM AND FAMILY

LEFT TO RIGHT: Paul Bentel; *The Fold*, 1980; Interior of St. Stephen the First Martyr Church (page 63); *Eye*, silkscreen, 1979, reissued as digital print, 2018; Wave chair, 1990

collages in wood and printmaking, a two-dimensional medium, which I used to represent the three-dimensional relationships of form and space I imagined. My love of bold contrast and vigorous pencil strokes served me well in figure drawing, a subject that also revealed the complex interactions of the surface or "skin" of an object and the internal shapes and forces it contains.

Graduate school in architecture followed immediately after college. At the time, the discussion in school centered on "Postmodernism" as a reaction against the Modernism I knew. It shocked me to encounter a design "discourse" so much at odds with my upbringing. In reaction, I studied the ways architecture reflects the ideas and values of those who make it. The people I knew designed and made the places where they lived. My work in school reflected my interest in building and culture both in the special projects I undertook, such as the publication, *Monumentality and the City*, which I co-edited as Harvard Architecture Review IV, and my work in the design studio.

Provoked in part by the disconnect between my understanding of architecture as an exercise in construction and the disembodied "theories" of architecture then prevailing in school and, in part, by my interest in the "culture" of architecture as a practice, I entered a doctoral program at MIT in History, Theory and Criticism of Architecture. I prepared my dissertation with Stanford Anderson and Leo Marx, a study of the transformation of American architecture practice in the 1920s and '30s. Through that project I learned the degree to which economic and political circumstances influence the professional discourse and thus how synthetic and arbitrary with respect to place and time design thinking can become. This experience reinforced my conviction that the practice of architecture must be circumscribed by the process of "making" buildings.

My training produced two primary, formal trajectories in my work: a craft-based/constructed vocabulary in which connections between articulated parts and materials are primary, and an aesthetic inspired by figure drawing, with fluid and seamless surfaces that are faired at structural transitions. I continue to study the ways buildings make culture manifest. I maintain the belief that architecture is an exercise in imagining simultaneously what to make and how to make it, a cultural practice of material transformation.

CORRELATIONS: LIFE + WORK BENTEL & BENTEL ARCHITECTS

PETER BENTEL, AIA

From my earliest days, I felt the pull between the solitary activities of drawing, painting, sculpture, and the communal activity of the theater. As I pursued these interests throughout high school, college, and beyond, I came to recognize architecture as an arena in which my interests across this range could be combined and cross-pollinated—one medium informing and enriching the others.

My parents encouraged creative engagements of any sort, which may explain why I cannot remember a time when I was not captivated by the arts. Their studio, where I spent every afternoon after school, lured me with its reams of large format paper, drafting tables and pencils to draw. In high school, my interests in visual arts (sculpture, mainly), creative writing (short story and poetry forms), and especially theater (both acting and set design) intensified. In those years, I became alert to the skills implicit to each as forms of artistic expression, as well as the power of their intermingling.

Among the fields of my early creative endeavors, theater offered the greatest insights into architecture as they both demand many talents and offer intense, all-encompassing experiences. I learned that acting is listening—listening to the other actors' characters to tune my response both to the playwright's words and to the emotional and physical context the actors are creating onstage. I recognize now that a significant part of my process of making architecture is listening—to the client (of course); to the location, the materials, the light; and to the movement through the site and building of people and natural phenomena such as sun and wind. As with the theater, architecture is shaping space, material and light into a four-dimensional experience that evokes feeling and emotion in those who engage with it.

At Princeton I met the teachers who would become mentors. The painter Sean Scully and the architect Michael Graves helped me understand the centrality of human experience—of both the artist and audience—to authentic artistic practice. Although the methods and languages of their work may seem contradictory, I drew connections between attributes that I saw as aligned. They both wanted their work to speak of the human condition with delight and awe. Scully's brushstrokes reveal his hesitations and thought processes, while Graves used the history and culture of architecture as a touchstone for his personal reflections on architectural form. I learned from them that it is through our bodies, through our senses and movements, that we are engaged in a situation rather than positioned as spectators.

The faculty at the Harvard Graduate School of Design provided less in the way of mentorship, or perhaps I was less inclined toward that kind of guidance. Rather, I was absorbed,

WHO WE ARE FIRM AND FAMILY

LEFT TO RIGHT: Peter Bentel; Pallet art, 1981; Craft restaurant column (page 94); Apella conference center (page 136); Bone sculpture, 1980

even intoxicated, by the parade of ideas and approaches to architecture espoused by the faculty and students, notably French poststructuralist philosophy or forms from the pre-modern history of architecture.

But I began to develop a concern that the push toward narrow, non-spatial ways of thinking was well-intended but superficial. Very few of those who promoted non-architectural disciplines as guidance for architecture had spent the time required to understand those disciplines. I, along with a few other equally frustrated students, reacted by joining the Harvard Architecture Review to explore what we broadly termed "the making of architecture." We were not concerned with particular forms or construction techniques but rather with how those forms and techniques come into being in the midst of what we saw as constantly shifting tensions and alliances between theory, history, and the act of shaping space, material, and light into architecture.

Fast forward three decades, my interests in the fine excess of form-making have been tempered by the appeal of sparseness, rigor, and an austere naturalness balanced by warmth, surprise, and humor. I continue to appreciate the innately collaborative process of designing and constructing architecture. In my work, I focus on the development of the character (of the buildings and interiors) we create. Character,

an admittedly elusive term, is the essence of a building or interior: its material, space, and light and also the vital qualities these together convey. I hope that the character of the architecture I am able to design—singly or in unison with others—possesses a vitality expressive of the creative act and equal to the lives of those who experience it.

CORRELATIONS: LIFE + WORK   BENTEL & BENTEL ARCHITECTS

CAROL RUSCHE BENTEL, FAIA

I was born into a large extended family in St. Louis, Missouri, and I grew up in a suburb of the city. My father worked in a paper factory, and I spent hours making things from the scraps he brought home. When I was nine, I was selected to dance in the St. Louis Municipal Opera production of *The Wizard of Oz* and continued to perform in the following seasons. Four years later, I started a dance studio in my parents' basement. Teaching and choreographing dance was my intended professional trajectory until a career questionnaire revealed that I should be an architect. I attended the only architecture program in Missouri, at Washington University, and among my professors there was Leslie Laskey, who studied under Laszlo Moholy-Nagy and taught at North Carolina State University prior to teaching the renowned preliminary design course at Washington University. I then pursued a Master of Architecture degree at North Carolina State University, where I studied under Roger Clark and Michael Pause—authors of the book *Precedents in Architecture*, to which I contributed. I decided that Boston was likely to have good opportunities in my chosen profession, and so, shortly after graduating, with my AIA Medal and Teaching Assistant Award in hand, I set out for the Northeast.

Within two weeks, I had been hired at The Architects Collaborative in Cambridge, where I worked under Sally Harkness. I absorbed a Modernist design approach and experienced a studio-style office. My next position was at Don Hisaka's office in Cambridge, a smaller firm where a single designer took charge of a project from start to finish. During that time, I met Paul Bentel in Cambridge. In 1984, we collaborated on what turned out to be one of eight winning projects for an ideas competition for Times Square, organized by the Municipal Art Society and the National Endowment for the Arts. Concurrently, I decided it was time to return to learning about and teaching architecture. I spent a year as an assistant professor at Georgia Tech and another year focused on architectural history and theory at the *Istituto Universitario di Architettura di Venezia* as a Fulbright Fellow. I studied with renowned theorist Manfredo Tafuri and eminent historian of Italian interwar architecture Giorgio Ciucci.

Paul and I got engaged in Italy in 1987, and we were married later that year, shortly after I joined what was then Paul's parents' firm, Bentel & Bentel. There I was happy to embrace the single-partner, beginning-to-end project responsibility as exemplified at Hisaka's office. I preferred the beginning and end to the middle, immersing myself in considering design alternatives in early stages and fine-tuning materials in late stages. But along the way I found art curation, a hallmark of our firm, to be especially satisfying. We introduce art early

WHO WE ARE FIRM AND FAMILY

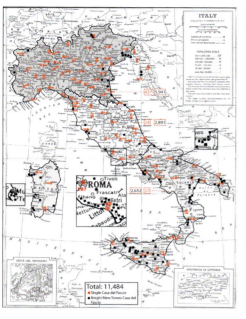

LEFT TO RIGHT: Carol Rusche Bentel; Dining booth at Rouge Tomate (page 107); Cor Jesu Academy (page 76); Map of *case del fascio* locations in Italy; Resource and Image Center, School of Visual Arts (page 88); Pascaline barstool designed by Bentel & Bentel

during the design process because it helps to define spaces and offers an intuitive wayfinding tool.

I mix practice with teaching, having learned from Maria and Fred Bentel's examples. I am currently Chair of the Interior Design: Built Environments Department at School of Visual Arts. Instead of hewing to the convention prevalent in most interior design schools—learning to fashion interiors for the well-off—I immerse students in current social issues, behavioral science, and the design of interiors for non-traditional recipients of design services. Focusing on the "inside" has reinforced my belief that as designers we have an essential role and a responsibility.

My contributions to our work are informed by my knowledge of architectural history and precedent, honed at NCSU, IAUV, the American Academy in Rome, and the Massachusetts Institute of Technology (MIT), where I received a doctorate in the history, theory, and criticism of art and architecture. Especially important in shaping my views were James Ackerman, for whom I worked in the Fine Arts Department at Harvard; Micha Bandini, who came to MIT from the Architectural Association in London to teach a course on Italian Modernism; and my many personal interviews with architects who practiced during the interwar period, such as Alberto Sartoris, Ignazio Gardella, Ludovico Belgiojoso, and Gino Pollini. Of particular value has been my three decades of research on architect Giuseppe Terragni and the Italian Modernists, from their fascination with glass to their ability to make buildings speak—more accurately, shout—about politics, which taught me that design can communicate without words and affect society in ways good and bad.

CORRELATIONS: LIFE + WORK BENTEL & BENTEL ARCHITECTS

INSTITUTIONAL IDENTITIES

From the earliest years, our practice has been centered around the design of religious buildings, schools, and libraries—in short, organizations that serve the larger community. Naturally, we devote careful attention to meeting the evolving functional needs detailed by our clients: religious protocols, specific teaching methods, new technologies, and special collections. But our larger mission, present in every decision we make, is to express institutional identity.

In many cases, our work for institutions involves additions to existing buildings—additions that can double (or more than double) usable space. We take one of two approaches toward this type of project: we introduce new architectural forms that complement existing ones and/or we defer to the material palette and details of the original structure.

WHO WE ARE   FIRM AND FAMILY: DESIGN PHILOSOPHY

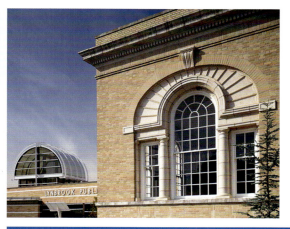

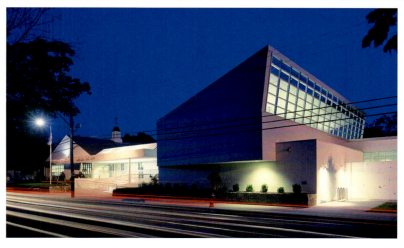

CLOCKWISE FROM TOP LEFT: Parish of the Holy Cross church (page 81); St. Stephen the First Martyr Church (page 63); Entrance to Old Westbury Hebrew Congregation, Old Westbury, New York, 2001; Lynbrook Public Library, Lynbrook, New York, 1992; Cor Jesu Academy (page 76); Massapequa Public Library, Massapequa, New York, 1997; Couch Academic Center, Webb Institute (page 173)

CORRELATIONS: LIFE + WORK BENTEL & BENTEL ARCHITECTS

HOSPITALITY DESTINATIONS

As our practice expanded into the hospitality realm in the 1990s, we looked to contribute not only to the specific destination but to the related streetscape. As we worked in this area, it became clear that restaurants and hotels would benefit from the kind of long-term planning decisions and attention to authenticity (in materials and details) we applied to our institutional work. The designs that emerge from this process are also more likely to be retained should ownership change.

WHO WE ARE   FIRM AND FAMILY: DESIGN PHILOSOPHY

CLOCKWISE FROM TOP LEFT: Gramercy Tavern (page 68); Toku restaurant, Manhasset, New York, 2006; Rouge Tomate Chelsea (page 162); The Modern restaurant (page 98); W Hotel Boston entrance (page 122); Hyatt Regency Chicago (page 152); Houston's restaurant, Boston, Massachusetts, 2003

CORRELATIONS: LIFE + WORK   BENTEL & BENTEL ARCHITECTS

INSIDE-OUTSIDE DIALOGUE

One feature of our design work is a conviction that exterior and interior are interdependent and equally critical. Where we can, we bring the outside world into our interiors and also reveal something of those interiors to the world outside. Admitting natural light by day and releasing artificial light by night can be key parts of this exchange.

WHO WE ARE   FIRM AND FAMILY: DESIGN PHILOSOPHY

FAR LEFT (TOP AND BOTTOM): The Hill Center, interior and exterior, St. Joseph's University, Brooklyn, New York, 2014 CLOCKWISE FROM LEFT: Cor Jesu Academy (page 76); Waldorf School (page 104); Lynbrook Public Library, Lynbrook, New York, 1992; Ground Café (page 149)

CORRELATIONS: LIFE + WORK   BENTEL & BENTEL ARCHITECTS

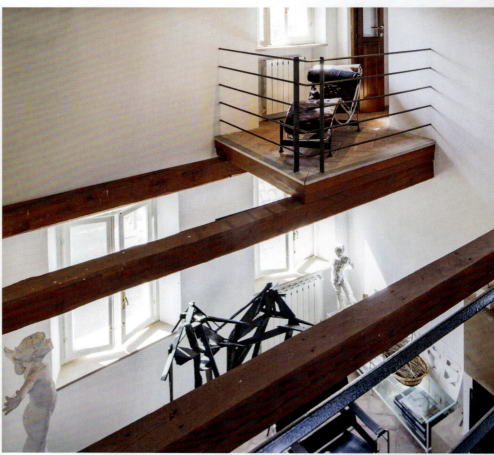
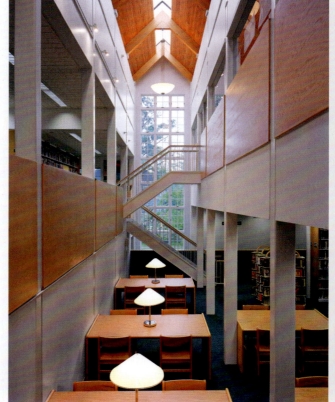

SPATIAL DRAMA

Dramatic interior views are possible within large volumes but also within relatively narrow confines. Vistas through to other parts of a building or between levels promote interior wayfinding and add spatial variety. Any loss of floor area is more than made up for by additional daylight and double-height spaces.

CLOCKWISE FROM TOP LEFT: Business Technology Center, St. Joseph's University, Patchogue, New York, 2002; Bentel house in Lucca, Italy (page 18); Hyatt Regency Chicago (page 152); Rouge Tomate (page 107); Oyster Bay Public Library, Oyster Bay, New York, 1993

WHO WE ARE   FIRM AND FAMILY: DESIGN PHILOSOPHY

CORRELATIONS: LIFE + WORK BENTEL & BENTEL ARCHITECTS

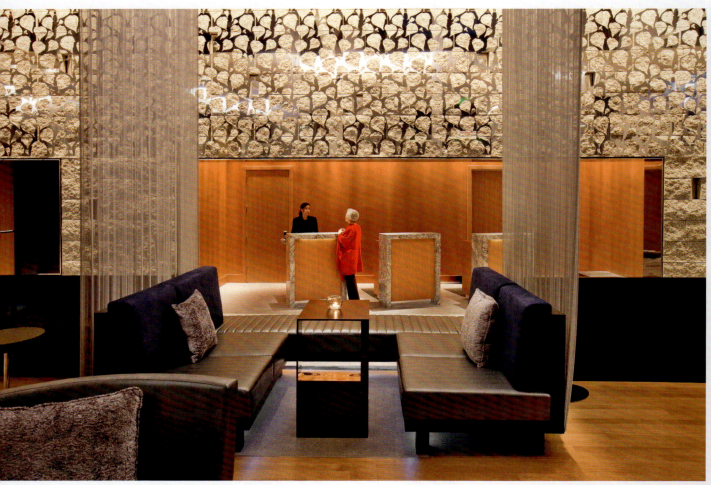

PATTERN AND TEXTURE

We use surface treatments to reinforce the identity of our interiors. The materials we select align with the essence of the project and, in many cases, are manually worked to show off their inherent characteristics. Reused barn boards, shimmering oyster shells, solid chunks of teak wood, and handcrafted leather may be appreciated by the hand as much as by the eye.

On occasion, the purpose of a project is best communicated by materials produced by modern fabrication processes. We have installed wall surfaces composed of singular or repeating patterns in Corten steel, light-diffusing disks, laser-cut reflective screens and suspended metal fixtures with irregular punched holes that emit light.

WHO WE ARE   FIRM AND FAMILY: DESIGN PHILOSOPHY

PAGE 42, CLOCKWISE FROM TOP LEFT: Lobby of W Hotel Boston (page 122); Bar ceiling at Hunter Restaurant (page 202); Barn wood wall at Rouge Tomate Chelsea (page 162); Translucent panel, Apella conference center (page 136); Teak wood screen at Le Bernardin (page 130); PAGE 43, CLOCKWISE FROM TOP RIGHT: Breakout space at Apella conference center (page 136); Leather wall at Craft (page 94); Oyster shell wall at Island Creek Oyster Bar, Boston, Massachusetts, 2013

CORRELATIONS: LIFE + WORK   BENTEL & BENTEL ARCHITECTS

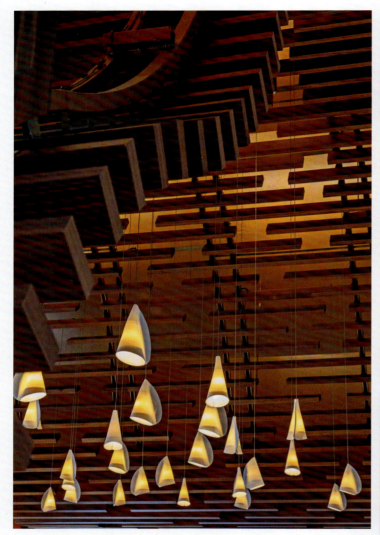

ATTENTION TO CEILINGS

We tend to focus more design effort on what is above than on what is below. Ceilings are complex, requiring the integration of acoustics, lighting, speakers, sprinklers, and air handling, much of which is magically hidden. Among the visually distinctive ceiling treatments we have devised are a repetitive surface of acoustic domes, a three-dimensional grid of fabric-wrapped panels recalling a Provençal picnic blanket, dense latticework with acoustic panels covered by copper screens, and wood ceiling panels that hide functional mechanics in irregular slits.

WHO WE ARE FIRM AND FAMILY: DESIGN PHILOSOPHY

CLOCKWISE FROM TOP LEFT: Hunter Restaurant (page 202); North End Grill, New York, 2012; Medí at Rockefeller Center, New York, 2001; Privé, New York, 2015; Colicchio & Sons, New York, 2010

CORRELATIONS: LIFE + WORK   BENTEL & BENTEL ARCHITECTS

SPACE DEFINED WITHOUT WALLS

Various settings call for delineating different areas without erecting walls or other barriers. We have used lit canopies, ceiling planes with contrasting colors or textures, and constellations of lights to identify interior spaces from above. Outdoors, built elements like shade sails and plant material are used to establish exterior rooms.

WHO WE ARE   FIRM AND FAMILY: DESIGN PHILOSOPHY

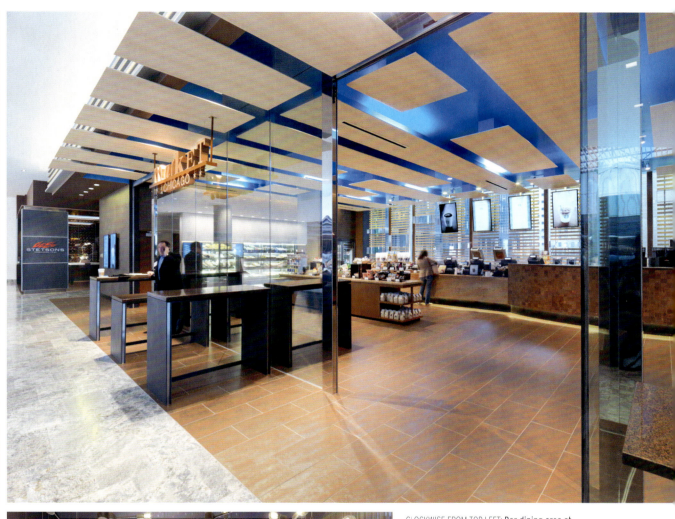

CLOCKWISE FROM TOP LEFT: Bar dining area at The Modern restaurant (page 98); Aldo Sohm Wine Bar, New York, 2015; Market shopping place at Hyatt Regency Chicago (page 152); Dining room at Hall Arts Hotel (page 184); Bentel house in Lucca, Italy (page 18); Gordon Ramsay restaurant at Heathrow Airport, London, 2008

CORRELATIONS: LIFE + WORK   BENTEL & BENTEL ARCHITECTS

SHAPING SPACE WITH LIGHT

Light is an essential material in all of our interiors. Raking light across interior wood wall surfaces evokes warmth and enhances the natural texture of the material. Dropping a horizontal grid of lights into a tall space makes a grand room more intimate. Illuminating a scrim at the window limits inward and softens outward views, ensuring that interiors are private—or just a bit public, as we modify the inward views by adjusting the intensity of the light.

WHO WE ARE FIRM AND FAMILY: DESIGN PHILOSOPHY

CLOCKWISE FROM TOP LEFT: Dining room at Club 432 (page 167); Hunter Restaurant (page 202); Dining spaces at Riverpark (page 136); Lighted window screening at Le Bernardin (page 130); Stairway lighting at Craft Atlanta, 2009; Uplit custom-designed wood screen at Le Bernardin (page 130)

CORRELATIONS: LIFE + WORK   BENTEL & BENTEL ARCHITECTS

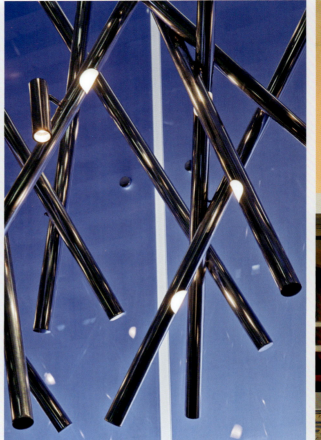

FOCUS ON THE DETAILS

Finely developed details have always been characteristic of our work. Framing and glazing—both clear and translucent—are boldly expressed in a rooftop light monitor. Aluminum tubes are assembled by the architects to form a lighting canopy, which provides both ambient and directional lighting. Small-scaled sills for narrow windows contribute to a distinctive façade pattern. Marble is made to appear thick and also curved, complementing the reflective oval ceiling cove above of a similar color. Metal accents join wood veneer in custom cabinetwork.

WHO WE ARE   FIRM AND FAMILY: DESIGN PHILOSOPHY

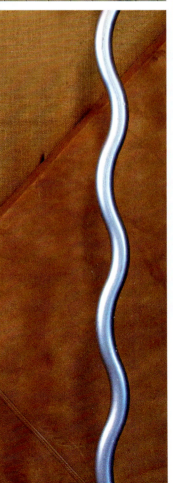

CLOCKWISE FROM TOP LEFT: Lynbrook Public Library, Lynbrook, New York, 1992; Aluminum light sculpture at Grand Hyatt Hotel (page 144); Cor Jesu Academy entry (page 76); Anthony's Bar, St. Louis, Missouri, 2021; Millwork at Eleven Madison Park (page 84)

CORRELATIONS: LIFE + WORK   BENTEL & BENTEL ARCHITECTS

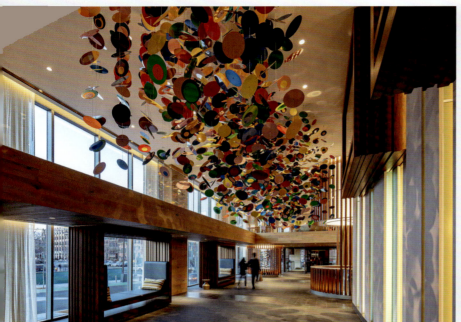

INTEGRATING ART

Artworks are fundamental components of our architecture. As part of the design process, we consider the form, content, physical attributes, and placement of art. We then find or commission works that fit our vision—in a few instances, art by members of our family. We might install sculpture to identify a key location, such as an entry, or to guide patrons in a particular direction. Suspended sculpture may serve as a ceiling that defines a space without enclosing it with walls. As we develop strategies for art pieces, we work closely with painters, sculptors, or photographers on the creation of specific works.

We use large murals and large-scale photography to expand space and to create windows where none exist. Often these two-dimensional works draw on colors from nature and serve as scenic backdrops. Sculpture may provide a focal point, fill a memorable niche, tell a particular story, or simply add delight. Lighting (from the back or above, internal, charged by the sun) is often tied to the artwork and its purpose in the space.

THIS PAGE (CLOCKWISE FROM TOP LEFT): 235 Grand lobby, Jersey City, New Jersey, Bentel collaboration with Ekko Mobiles, 2019; Terroir TriBeCa, Galileo Pavilion, New York, Michela Bentel & Fuad Khazam, 2021; Sculpture by Deborah Butterfield at Houston's restaurant, Boston, Massachusetts, 2001; Sculptures *Awilda* and *Chloe* by Jaume Plensa, Grand Hyatt Hotel lobby (page 144); Sculpture by Damon Hyldreth at Hudson Yards Grill (page 192)

WHO WE ARE   FIRM AND FAMILY: DESIGN PHILOSOPHY

THIS PAGE (CLOCKWISE FROM TOP LEFT): *Photosynthesis 8:31* by Per Fronth above entry passage at Rouge Tomate Chelsea (page 162); Thomas Demand photographic mural *Clearing* at The Modern restaurant (page 98); Solar-powered *Spice Towers* by Michela Bentel at Hunter Restaurant (page 202); *James' Flowers* mural by America Martin, Tony's restaurant, St. Louis, Missouri, 2021; Glass cones by the architects at Café Vettro, Las Vegas, Nevada, 2009; *Walking Horizons* painting by Burghard Müller-Dannhausen at Grand Hyatt Hotel (page 144)

CORRELATIONS: LIFE + WORK   BENTEL & BENTEL ARCHITECTS

BEYOND THE BUILDING

Master planning operates on a scale much grander than that of most of our work. Designs for a campus or a community typically address acres of space and take into account current needs as well as those far in the future. We strive for consistency in placing buildings and in selecting construction materials. We shape exterior spaces, often as outdoor rooms. Our planning responds to the context and terrain and to the color and texture of existing architecture.

WHO WE ARE   FIRM AND FAMILY: DESIGN PHILOSOPHY

TOP ROW FROM FAR LEFT: Waldorf School library (page 104); *(top)* Waldorf School campus plan; *(bottom)* Couch Academic Center addition to master plan at Webb Institute (page 173); Couch Academic Center, Webb Institute (page 173) MIDDLE ROW (LEFT TO RIGHT): New public library, Oakland Park (page 212); High school addition for Cor Jesu Academy (page 76) BOTTOM ROW (LEFT TO RIGHT): Campus view with new student union for St. Joseph's University in Patchogue under construction; Campus plan for Cor Jesu Academy (page 76)

55

CORRELATIONS: LIFE + WORK BENTEL & BENTEL ARCHITECTS

EXTENDING THE PRACTICE

All of the Bentels have held academic appointments: Maria (New York Institute of Technology), Fred (Pratt University, New York Institute of Technology), Paul (Columbia, Harvard, ETH Zurich, and elsewhere), Peter (New York School of Interior Design), and Carol (currently chair of the undergraduate interior design program at the School of Visual Arts; formerly New York Institute of Technology, Harvard, and elsewhere). Linking teaching with practice allows us to inform young designers about the realities of practicing architecture and interior design; at the same time, it strengthens our connections to the issues that concern current generations of students, such as sustainability, social equity, and technology. We have taught a wide variety of subjects: design studio, architectural history and theory, library design, hospitality design, historic preservation, and specific topics such as American and Italian Modernism. Our 2018 book, *Nourishing the Senses: Restaurant Architecture of Bentel & Bentel,* presented our work and thoughts on hospitality design.

WHO WE ARE   FIRM AND FAMILY: DESIGN PHILOSOPHY

OPPOSITE TOP LEFT: Bentel articles and book
LEFT: Carol Rusche Bentel at School of Visual Arts in Manhattan
ABOVE (TOP TO BOTTOM): Paul Bentel with students in Lucca, Italy; Carol Rusche Bentel in project critique at School of Visual Arts with guest critic and Master Sommelier Pascaline Lepeltier

CORRELATIONS: LIFE + WORK   BENTEL & BENTEL ARCHITECTS

THE NEXT GENERATION

Michela, Nikolas, and Lukas (Paul and Carol's children), and Antonia (Peter's daughter) grew up, as Paul and Peter did, in the architecture studio. They absorbed the art of making, mostly in three dimensions, from parents and grandparents. Two of the four are studying architecture, perhaps leading to the next generation of our family firm.

WHO WE ARE FIRM AND FAMILY: THE NEXT GENERATION

TOP (LEFT TO RIGHT): Michela with *Steel Forest* sculpture, 2013; Michela's spoon sculpture *Sperm and Egg*, 2014; Nikolas with his chalk toys; Lukas carving marble in Lucca, Italy; Lukas with ice sculpture in the Adirondacks
BOTTOM (LEFT TO RIGHT): Four Bentel cousins in Italy, 1997; Lukas and Nikolas at family's Locust Valley sculpture studio, 1997; Antonia with artwork; Lukas's sculpture of Nikolas in Orchard House; Bentel children in art studio in Lucca, Italy

WHAT WE DO

ST. STEPHEN THE FIRST MARTYR CHURCH

Warwick, New York | 1991

During the late twentieth century, the population of the suburbs around New York City grew rapidly and with it the demand for religious buildings. The first generation of Bentel & Bentel designed numerous churches for locations on Long Island and in the Hudson Valley. The second generation played major roles as designers of the later religious buildings, most significantly for the design of St. Stephen the First Martyr Church, completed in 1991.

Located in the rolling farmland of Orange County, New York, St. Stephen combines the rationality and clarity of twentieth-century Modern design with the warmth of color and texture associated with Roman Catholic ritual. The axial form of the principal worship space, with its steep roof, recalls historic church forms yet also shares a kinship with the barns and other farm outbuildings of this area, which share a similar exposure of structure and economy of means.

The site's specimen trees and "plantation" of red pines inspired a distinctive structural device. The columns supporting the church's roof sprout clusters of branches, as do the pines, in this case reaching out to support the roof beams.

The layout of the chancel and seating in the main sanctuary, for up to seven hundred worshipers, reflects Roman Catholic planning principles of the time. A smaller atrium at the entry serves as a secular gathering place and can accommodate one hundred congregants under its raised roof.

The new church is one element in a complex of buildings that includes an existing school and a new sacristy and parish center designed by the firm, which were to harmonize with the church yet express their own scale and character both inside and out.

St. Stephen won the 1995 National Religious Architecture Award.

CORRELATIONS: LIFE + WORK BENTEL & BENTEL ARCHITECTS

WHAT WE DO ST. STEPHEN THE FIRST MARTYR CHURCH

CORRELATIONS: LIFE + WORK   BENTEL & BENTEL ARCHITECTS

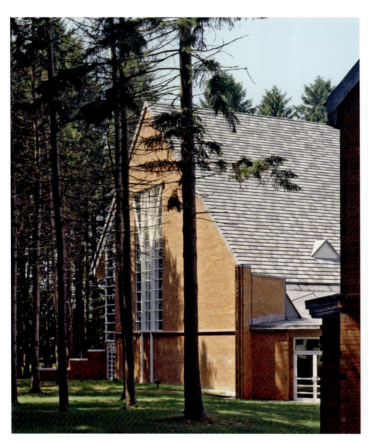

WHAT WE DO ST. STEPHEN THE FIRST MARTYR CHURCH

PAGES 62-63: Church seen from entry drive
PREVIOUS PAGES: Sanctuary with view into pines
LEFT: Hand-colored drawing of east elevation
BOTTOM (LEFT TO RIGHT): East end of sanctuary;
Exterior window detail; Tabernacle between
sanctuary columns

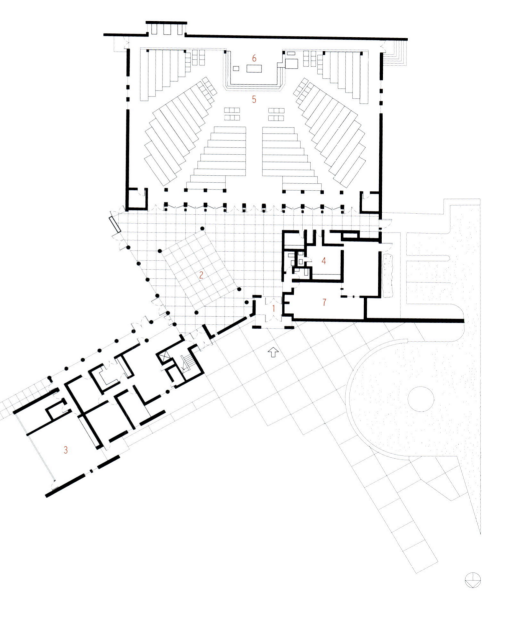

1 ENTRY
2 ATRIUM
3 PARISH OFFICES
4 SACRISTY
5 MAIN SANCTUARY
6 ALTAR
7 MEETING ROOM

CORRELATIONS: LIFE + WORK   BENTEL & BENTEL ARCHITECTS

ABOVE (LEFT TO RIGHT): View into Gramercy Tavern from street; Bar area OPPOSITE: Dining areas seen from bar
FOLLOWING PAGE (TOP TO BOTTOM): Bar area; Dining spaces defined by arched openings

GRAMERCY TAVERN

New York, New York | 1994

The first all-new restaurant the Bentel firm designed for the trend-setting restaurateur Danny Meyer, Gramercy Tavern, married the genteel traditions of the Gramercy Park neighborhood with up-to-the-minute concepts of food and drink service. Installed within an old industrial building is a series of spatial episodes inspired by historic taverns, which explore distinctions between the rustic and the refined, the provincial and the urbane.

The lofty and open ground floor of the former factory, with its grid of terra-cotta-covered columns and tall windows looking to the street, was used to advantage in the bar area just inside the entrance. A mural painting by the artist Robert Kushner, playfully representing a cornucopia of fruits and vegetables, corresponds to the transom windows of the building façade. The curve of the long bar meets the needs of the servers within and generates a sense of conviviality among the patrons who could more easily face one another. Nonstructural beams applied to the ceiling and a random variety of furniture, selected as if it had accumulated over a long period, underscore the tavern atmosphere.

The open industrial setting was less innately suited to smaller-scale dining environments beyond the bar, and so the scale is reduced toward the rear. These more intimate dining areas are organized as separate and varied spaces—none more than three tables across—by means of nonstructural columns, arches, and vaults. Artworks allude to popular history while also marking axes and reinforcing design symmetries.

Danny Meyer's restaurants are known for their warm hospitality. Here, the trait is combined with a welcoming tavern environment within a revered neighborhood, yielding a dining institution that has thrived, with no substantial alterations, for an exceptionally long time.

WHAT WE DO GRAMERCY TAVERN

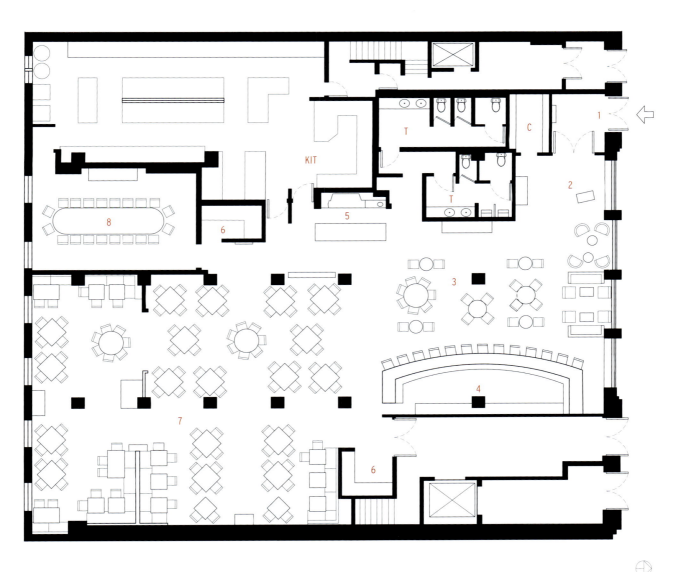

1 ENTRY
2 GREETER
3 CASUAL DINING
4 BAR
5 WOOD GRILL
6 BEVERAGE/SERVICE
7 DINING
8 PRIVATE DINING
C COATS
T TOILETS
KIT KITCHEN

BETHPAGE PUBLIC LIBRARY

BETHPAGE, NEW YORK | 2004

This public library is one of several designed by Bentel & Bentel for Long Island communities around the year 2000. At Bethpage, the project encompassed a thorough renovation of the original building and a large addition (larger in area than the original). The existing interior was reorganized to accommodate staff areas, children's library, and media rooms, while the addition included much-enlarged stacks for the adult collection, gallery space, a 240-seat auditorium, and light-filled reading areas.

The new functions reflect the evolving role of public libraries, which have become community spaces as well as book repositories. The auditorium and the gallery are located so that they can remain accessible to the public when other library rooms are closed.

The addition includes a new public façade with a glass-walled entrance area juxtaposed to the masonry-walled face of the auditorium. A generous entry canopy on one side and the auditorium volume on the other both angle gently in relation to the street, encouraging movement toward the central entrance.

The Grumman Corporation, a major producer of civilian and military aircraft, is Bethpage's major employer and taxpayer. The library's angular, winglike roof configurations subtly symbolize Grumman's role in the region. The roof projections are functional as well, blocking direct sunlight from entering indoor reading areas yet allowing generous outward views. A model of the Apollo Lunar Excursion Module sits in the heart of the library under the roof forms emphasizing the community's contributions to aeronautical exploration.

A new enclosed garden adjoining the auditorium serves as a convenient outdoor reading space and also an open-air reception and performance area. Tall brick walls and a transparent canopy ensure a feeling of seclusion. Custom wood seating was designed by the Bentel firm.

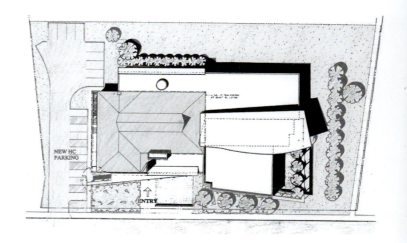

ABOVE: Site plan
OPPOSITE (TOP TO BOTTOM): Front of library; Entry canopy and light monitor

WHAT WE DO BETHPAGE PUBLIC LIBRARY

CORRELATIONS: LIFE + WORK   BENTEL & BENTEL ARCHITECTS

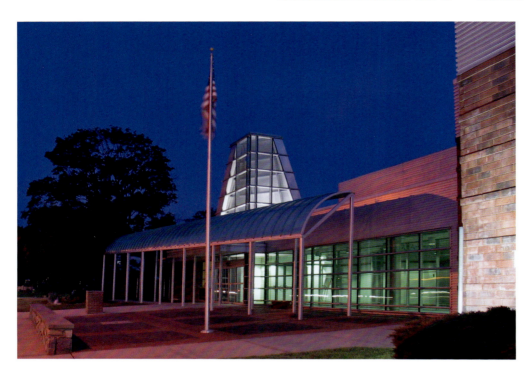

LEFT: Library front after dark
OPPOSITE (TOP TO BOTTOM): Reading garden;
Sunlit reading room

1 ENTRY
2 GALLERY
3 STAFF OFFICES
4 DIRECTOR OFFICE
5 LOUNGE
6 MEDIA STACKS
7 CIRCULATION DESK
8 CHILDREN'S LIBRARY
9 CHILDREN'S THEATER
10 ADULT LIBRARY STACKS
11 COMPUTER ROOM
12 REFERENCE
13 READING ROOM
14 THEATER
15 OUTDOOR READING GARDEN

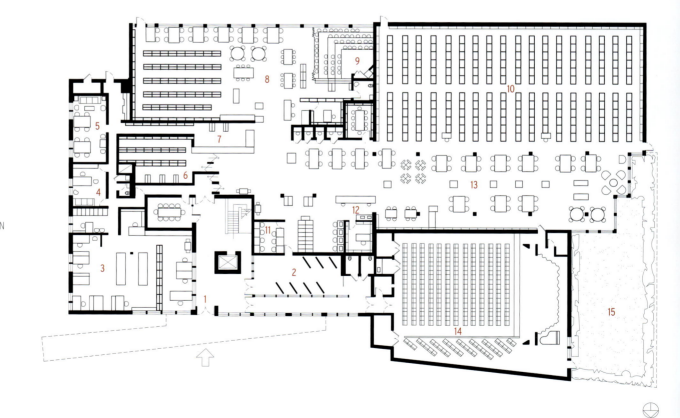

CORRELATIONS: LIFE + WORK   BENTEL & BENTEL ARCHITECTS

COR JESU ACADEMY

St. Louis, Missouri | 2005

TOP (LEFT TO RIGHT): Limestone wall detail; Stairwell wall seen from plaza; Tower with rainwater spout and catch basin
BELOW RIGHT: Plaza enclosed by lighted public spaces

The addition to a private, college-preparatory high school for girls in the St. Louis suburbs achieved a number of goals. In addition to increasing the school's capacity, it created a public identity for the academy on its hilltop location, facing a prominent street. It also provided a clearly visible public entry for a school that previously had several equal access points that were difficult for the public to discern.

The new entry took the form of a tower, with a distinctive silhouette related to the crest of the order of Catholic sisters who teach there, an abstracted reference to the heart of Jesus. The tower is not only prominently visible to the public but can be seen from much of the original building and from the glass-walled, single-loaded corridor that serves the addition, helping to orient students and visitors. Facilities in the 16,000-square-foot addition include five state-of-the-art classrooms, a large board room, and administrative offices.

The original 1957 school was organized around a courtyard, and the L shape of the addition creates a new, larger and more accessible "outdoor room" between the school's two construction phases. A curving red wall linking the new to the old, called the "Spirit Wall," is clearly visible from that outdoor space through a glazed corridor wall. The grand stair that connects the addition's two floors runs along a window wall and has niches for sculpture.

The addition is clad in brick and limestone that matches the exterior of the original building. Its interiors have terrazzo floors with embedded fragments of mother-of-pearl, which is featured in the school's class rings.

Other renovations carried out throughout the campus include a new parking lot, with underground water retainage and student drop-off, a rally amphitheater, and a "history path."

WHAT WE DO   COR JESU ACADEMY

CORRELATIONS: LIFE + WORK   BENTEL & BENTEL ARCHITECTS

LEFT: Classroom
OPPOSITE (TOP TO BOTTOM): View from upper corridor toward tower; Stairwell

1 ENTRY
2 FRONT PLAZA
3 TOWER
4 COURTYARD
5 PLAZA
6 CONFERENCE ROOM
7 FACULTY OFFICE
8 CLASSROOM
9 OFFICES
10 STAFF AREA
11 RAIN BASIN

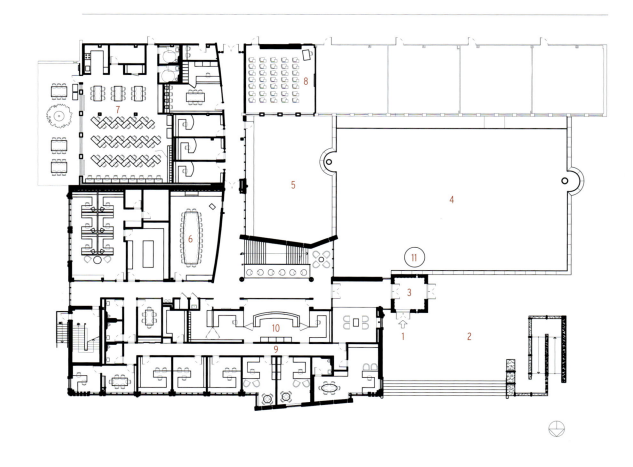

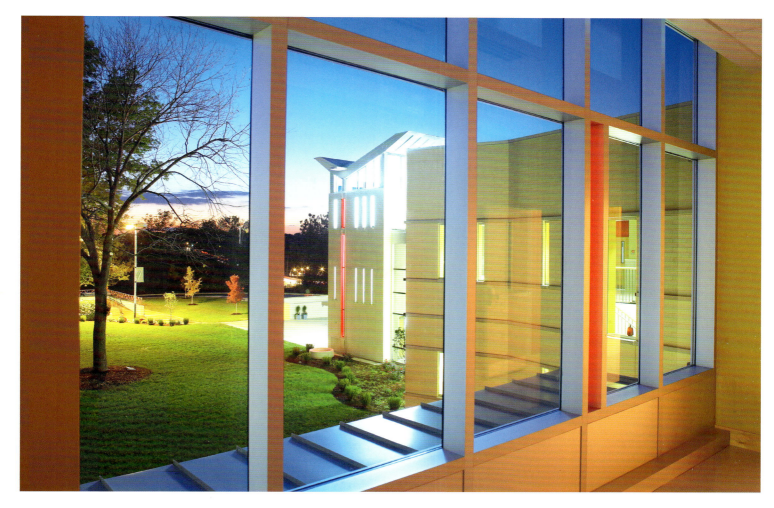

PARISH OF THE HOLY CROSS

Nesconset, New York | 1995

The new church was placed at the high point of a 4.5-acre site dotted with characteristic Eastern Long Island pin oaks and scrub pines. Since the site slopes sharply up from the road, it was decided to locate most of the parking around its perimeter, with a wide buffer of trees surrounding the church itself. As parishioners arrive at the site, they can view the detached bell tower rising above the treetops, drawing them to the entry. The wooded slopes act as a filter between the world below and the sacred precinct of the worship space, with an additional courtyard buffer at the entry.

The colonnaded courtyard provides the worshippers' first gathering place. Above this enclosure rises the sharply angular volume of the sanctuary, its dramatic structural system visible through ascending triangles of glass enclosure. Inside the main sanctuary, up to 575 worshippers can be accommodated on three sides of the altar platform, encouraging a more open worship experience. The prominent structural elements supporting the sharply peaked sanctuary roof take the form of four white steel "trees," which bring the forest indoors and recall the inventive vaulting of Gothic churches as well as the outstretched arms of Christ on the cross.

A spacious interior narthex accommodates up to 400 participants for non-worship events, as well as overflow seating for masses at Christmas and Easter. The design of other auxiliary components of the church—including a daily chapel, sacristy, and offices—repeat some of the church's characteristic peaks and glazed triangles at a smaller scale. Throughout every space, the design maintains a consistent palette of simple materials—black slate floors, white stucco walls, and cedar clapboard ceilings—reinforcing the idea that all parts of a parish church are integral to the religious experience.

CORRELATIONS: LIFE + WORK   BENTEL & BENTEL ARCHITECTS

WHAT WE DO   PARISH OF THE HOLY CROSS

PREVIOUS PAGES: Sanctuary seen from entry courtyard
TOP (LEFT TO RIGHT): Church seen from arrival drive; Tower and entry court; Interior corridor; Baptismal font with altar beyond
BELOW LEFT: Sanctuary with tree-like columns

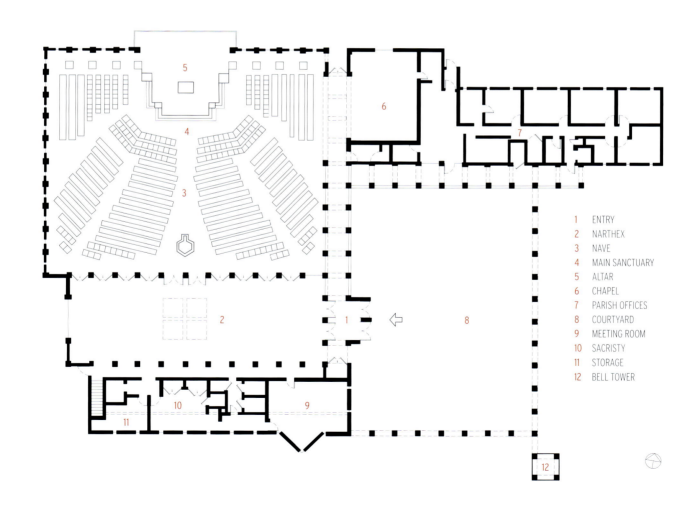

1   ENTRY
2   NARTHEX
3   NAVE
4   MAIN SANCTUARY
5   ALTAR
6   CHAPEL
7   PARISH OFFICES
8   COURTYARD
9   MEETING ROOM
10   SACRISTY
11   STORAGE
12   BELL TOWER

ELEVEN MADISON PARK

New York, New York | 1996

TOP (LEFT TO RIGHT): Building seen from Madison Square Park; Restaurant entry through building's arcade; Main dining room with view into park; Model of tower's original design
BELOW RIGHT: Main dining room with preserved details of former banking hall

The setting for what has become one of New York's most celebrated restaurants was the soaring former banking hall at the base of the Metropolitan Life building. Prominently rising along Madison Square Park, this Art Deco tower is recognized both as an official city landmark and on the National Register of Historic Places.

The design challenge here was to take full advantage of this grand volume while creating more intimate "communities" of tables within it. A key decision was to raise the floor level in about half of the room, dividing it into two spaces of more hospitable dimensions. Consistency of furnishings and details kept either area from appearing the more desirable of the two.

Though the room volume and its ceiling detailing were impressive, the existing floors were of bare concrete. The architects designed new terrazzo flooring with the angular patterns and subtly offbeat colors characteristic of Art Deco. The wood surfaces of the low partitions and cabinetry that were designed to divide the space were ornamented with abstract depictions of leaves from Madison Park's venerable trees, visible through the room's tall windows.

Preservation regulations delayed installation of down-lights in the room's ceiling, so the architects designed light-supporting hoops suspended around the existing period chandeliers. After this limitation expired at the end of five years, these were replaced with recessed down-lighting.

A low-ceilinged bar and third dining area adjoining the main space provided two related, but alternative, environments. Contrasting in their atmosphere, the gilded angular planes on the ceiling of the bar made the area festive, while historical photos of buildings surrounding Madison Park were located at the head height of diners seated in the cozier dining area, stressing its intimacy. Private dining spaces on the mezzanine above offered generous views of the dining room and the park beyond.

Eleven Madison Park won best design of the year from IIDA. In 2017, the restaurant was rated Number 1 in the listing World's 50 Best Restaurants.

WHAT WE DO   ELEVEN MADISON PARK

CORRELATIONS: LIFE + WORK   BENTEL & BENTEL ARCHITECTS

TOP (LEFT TO RIGHT): Bar room; Dining area; Custom lighting at bar
OPPOSITE: Bar area with faceted ceiling

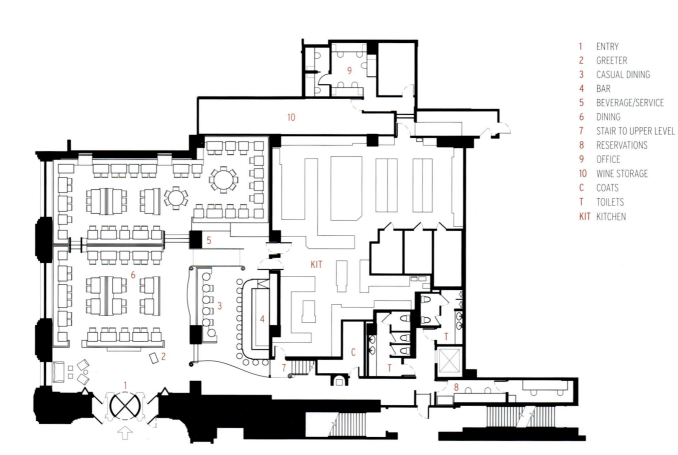

1 ENTRY
2 GREETER
3 CASUAL DINING
4 BAR
5 BEVERAGE/SERVICE
6 DINING
7 STAIR TO UPPER LEVEL
8 RESERVATIONS
9 OFFICE
10 WINE STORAGE
C COATS
T TOILETS
KIT KITCHEN

RESOURCE AND IMAGE CENTER, SVA

New York, New York | 2000

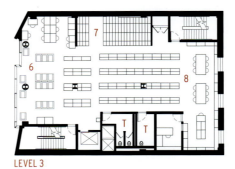

1	ENTRY
2	GALLERY
3	THEATER
4	READING ROOM
5	CIRCULATION DESK
6	READING LOUNGE
7	COMPACT SHELVING
8	GENERAL STACKS
T	TOILETS

LEVEL 3

LEVEL 2

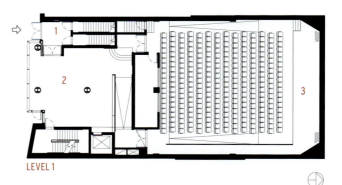

LEVEL 1

The proposed building would be the first purpose-built structure for the eminent School of Visual Arts (SVA), which occupies a variety of adapted buildings in Midtown Manhattan. Intended to centralize SVA's resources of visual materials for both the school and the surrounding city, the building was designed to house a vast collection of illustration art, comics, posters, and movie scripts, as well as a computer graphics lab, an auditorium/cinema, and gallery spaces.

The site was a vacant fifty-foot by 100-foot lot on a side street. The challenge was to fit the program in a seven-story structure. The first floor would have a generous glass-walled lobby along the street and an auditorium/cinema extending to the back of the property. Upper floors would have smaller footprints to meet zoning requirements and assure adequate light and air for both this structure and its neighbors.

The design of the building's street front presented an especially interesting challenge. There was inevitably a desire for the structure to present an identifiable face to the city, within its narrow confines. But most of the library functions and its collections required interiors without windows.

The design solution involved placing reading rooms along the street frontage and enclosing them with areas of clear and frosted glass. The face of the building was boldly organized around a central rectangle clad in various types of glass, framed by largely solid areas clad in copper and stone. As sunlight faded at the end of each day, ambient light from the reading spaces would transform the façade into a distinctive source of diffused light. The use of fine varieties of glass, patinated copper, and stone would give the center a gravitas appropriate to the institution it was meant to represent. The project received zoning approval and a building permit.

OPPOSITE: Hand-drawn front elevation

WHAT WE DO RESOURCE AND IMAGE CENTER, SVA

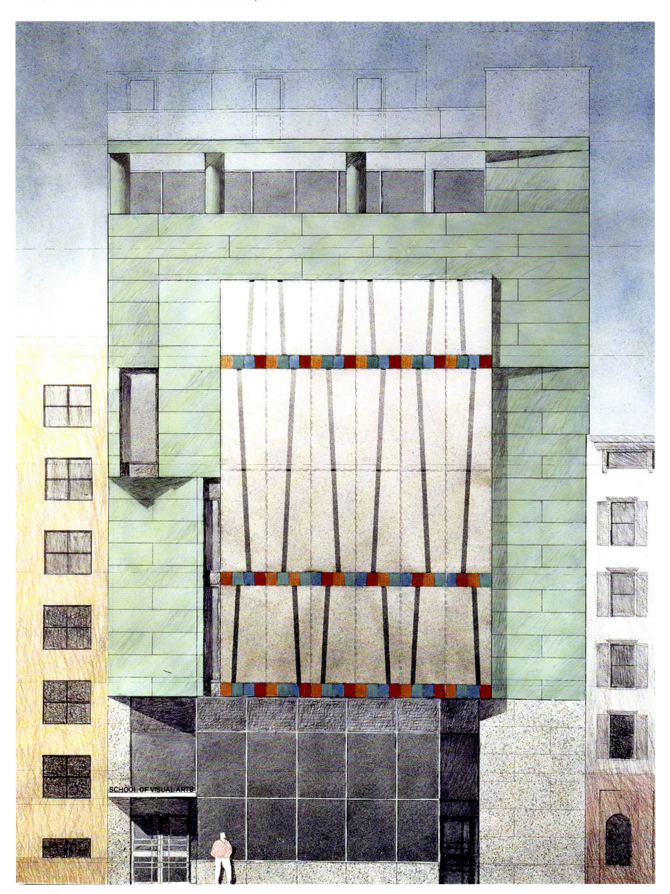

CHARAPANI

Dover Plains, New York | 2002

Set on 85 acres of former farmland, this Dutchess County retreat—named Charapani by its owners—was designed to mediate between a forest edge at the top of a hill and the open fields that slope away to the southwest. The dense growth of trees would provide a barrier against northerly winds and an intimacy of setting, while the fields crossed by stone walls would offer stunning views of deep valleys and low mountains to the south. The narrowness of the house's plan, running along the forest-field boundary, would allow each of its rooms to share these contrasting natural environments.

In the house's construction, long walls of stone culled from the site would be woven between a grid of massive steel columns formed from intersecting I-beams, metaphorically combining the two aspects of the site. Proceeding from the entry court to the north, one could meander through the main living spaces toward the fields. Alternatively, one could move to one of the elevated spaces at either end of the house: the meditation space to the east or the guest quarters, above the swimming pool, to the west.

Rolling roof forms, clad in lead-coated copper applied to a warped, coffered structural grid, would echo the silhouettes of the distant landscape to the south while corresponding approximately to the heights of the tree canopy. Large expanses of glass would allow seamless transitions to the natural settings in both directions. The entire south wall of the main pavilion would lower into the cellar to reinforce the connection to nature. Broad overhangs would protect the interior from direct sunlight, rain, or snow. A simple material vocabulary of exposed steel, glass, plaster, and bubinga (West African rosewood) paneling—with straw mat flooring in the guest quarters—would provide a warm, serene setting for the occupants' engagement with the surrounding environment.

CORRELATIONS: LIFE + WORK BENTEL & BENTEL ARCHITECTS

PREVIOUS PAGES: **House at top of slope**
LEFT: **House with pool**
OPPOSITE (TOP TO BOTTOM): **East-west section; Model; House seen from entry court**

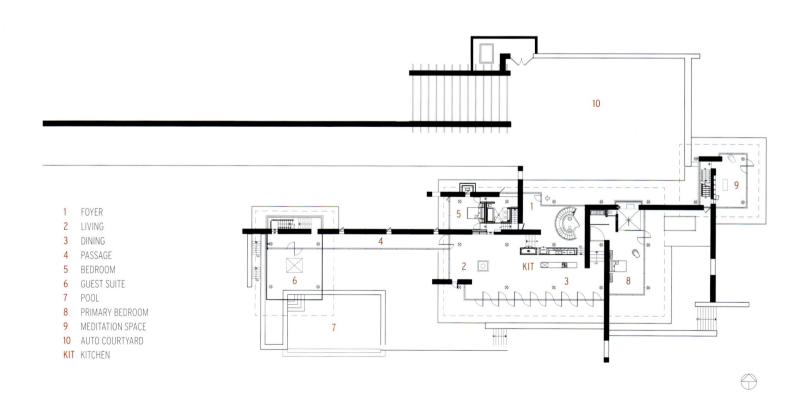

1 FOYER
2 LIVING
3 DINING
4 PASSAGE
5 BEDROOM
6 GUEST SUITE
7 POOL
8 PRIMARY BEDROOM
9 MEDITATION SPACE
10 AUTO COURTYARD
KIT KITCHEN

WHAT WE DO   CHARAPANI

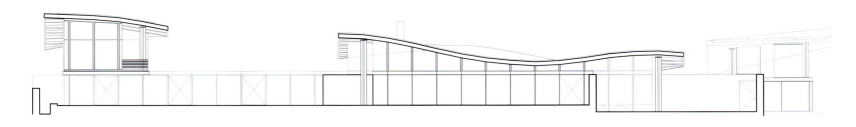

CRAFT

New York, New York | 2001

Craft was the first of several restaurants Bentel & Bentel would design for innovative chef Tom Colicchio, its name embodying his approach to cooking and serving. Tom believes that cooking is a craft, not an art–that it should bring out the innate flavors of seasonal ingredients and that each food should be served on a separate plate to be shared by the table.

Bentel & Bentel's design approach for Craft is, in a sense, a metaphor for Colicchio's principles regarding food and service. The inherent characteristics of the initial space are retained, its essential materials plainly exposed. Any added features are in uncoated materials, encouraged to show the mellowing effects of age.

In this instance, the fourteen-foot columns of the nineteenth-century mercantile building were stripped to reveal the terra-cotta block originally laid up as fire protection for the steel members inside them. A two-tiered wine vault was assembled of exposed steel and bronze. The wall facing it, curved to accommodate functional needs behind it, was clad in natural-colored leather applied with visible bronze fasteners.

The eighty-foot depth of the space is divided into zones more to less public by the carefully modulated narrowing between the curved leather wall and the wine vault, the constriction mitigated by the suggested pliability of one and penetrability of the other. The tall, deep space is made more intimate by its clusters of suspended exposed-filament lights. At the far end a painting by Stephen Hannock, extending entirely across the back wall, entitled *Squid Boats on the Gulf of Siam*, in effect opens up the room to a night view with flashes of bright light.

Bentel & Bentel went on to design other Craft restaurants in Atlanta, Dallas, and Los Angeles, all of which possess a similar rich materiality.

Craft won the 2002 National AIA Honor Award.

WHAT WE DO CRAFT

PREVIOUS PAGES: Restaurant seen from entry area
OPPOSITE: Leather wall
TOP (LEFT TO RIGHT): Custom-designed table; Detail of two-story wine rack; Bar

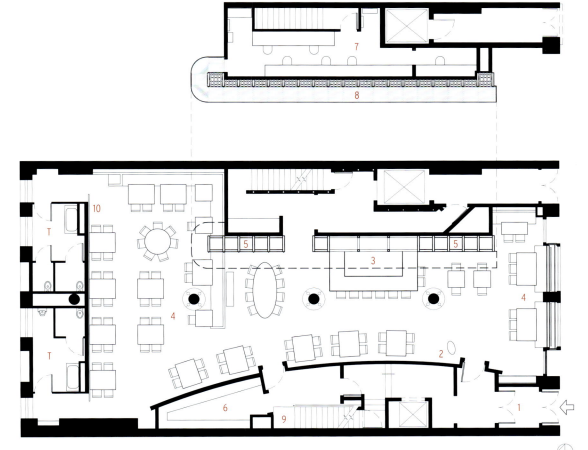

1 ENTRY
2 GREETER
3 BAR
4 DINING
5 WINE RACK
6 BEVERAGE/SERVICE STATION
7 UPSTAIRS OFFICE
8 WINE STORAGE CATWALK
9 ACCESS TO KITCHEN BELOW
10 ART WALL
T TOILETS

97

THE MODERN

New York, New York | 2005

TOP (LEFT TO RIGHT): Front of MoMA, restaurant entrance in foreground; Doors to restaurant; Bar
BELOW RIGHT: Casual dining area

When New York's Museum of Modern Art carried out its 2004 expansion, designed by architect Yoshio Taniguchi, it tapped the celebrated talents of restaurateur Danny Meyer for its expanded food services. And it enlisted, as well, the proven restaurant-design skills of Bentel & Bentel for those facilities—thus continuing an architect-restaurateur collaboration that had been notably successful at restaurants such as Gramercy Tavern and Eleven Madison Park.

The largest of the museum's dining places they created is The Modern, located on the first floor with its own street entrance so that it can be open beyond museum hours—and be a destination in itself. Its 322 seats are clearly divided between a bar-and-casual-dining area and a separate fine-dining space with its own menu. There is also a private dining room seating up to sixty-four, which can be divided in two.

A major asset of the assigned space is a view of the museum's landmark sculpture garden through a seventy-five-foot-long glass wall, now a singular feature of the fine-dining space. Its plan is organized so that no seat faces directly away from the garden. This area also includes the restaurant's highest ceiling, featuring a band of skylights.

Lending distinction to the internally focused casual dining area is a photomural *Clearing* by artist Thomas Demand—in effect opening an entire wall to a forest scene—and a canopy of reflective PVC panels that make the low ceiling seem higher. To guide visitors in through confined corridors from either the street or the museum, the architects designed sinuous walls of backlit white translucent glass, whose curved form is repeated on the fronts of the greeting desk and bar—all inspired by the museum's signature curved entrance canopy. The white glass walls slide by the bronze glass wine rack that repeats the color of the glass of MoMA's annex, which houses the kitchen.

The Modern won a 2006 James Beard Award for restaurant design and the 2007 National AIA Honor Award.

WHAT WE DO   THE MODERN

CORRELATIONS: LIFE + WORK BENTEL & BENTEL ARCHITECTS

WHAT WE DO   THE MODERN

OPPOSITE (CLOCKWISE FROM TOP LEFT): Lounge seating with Thomas Demand's photographic mural *Clearing*; Passage to private dining room; Pivoting doors to private dining room; Casual dining area with mural
TOP: Bar and glass wine rack

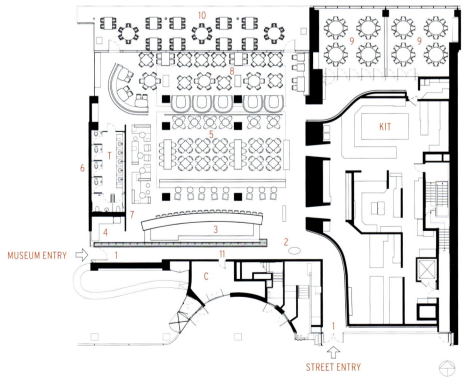

1   ENTRY
2   GREETER
3   BAR
4   BEVERAGE STATION
5   CASUAL DINING
6   ART WALL #1
7   ART WALL #2
8   FINE DINING
9   PRIVATE DINING
10 OUTDOOR TERRACE
11 WINE STORAGE
KIT KITCHEN
C   COATS
T   TOILETS

101

WHAT WE DO THE MODERN

OPPOSITE: Fine dining area
TOP TO BOTTOM: Dining terrace seen from MoMA sculpture garden;
Fine dining area with view of sculpture garden

CORRELATIONS: LIFE + WORK   **BENTEL & BENTEL ARCHITECTS**

ABOVE (LEFT TO RIGHT): Circulation desk area; Individual reading room
BELOW RIGHT: Library seen from school courtyard

MILLER LIBRARY, WALDORF SCHOOL

Garden City, New York | 2008

Constructing the Miller Library was one phase in the ongoing execution of the Waldorf School's master plan. The original school was a group of separate buildings connected by exterior arcades. The building units were built of brick with distinctive coursing and with hipped roofs that created the image of a peaceful village.

The overall design goal for this phase was to subtly connect the parts and to enclose the walkway system. These steps addressed the school's security concerns and the need to identify a single entry point. New windows and doors were installed throughout, the entrance was upgraded with a new central desk, and the high school was refurbished. The work was done with limited funds and with the involvement of the Waldorf community.

The Miller Library renovation and expansion was the largest part of this effort, nearly doubling the library space. A major design goal was to respect the existing "village" architecture while adding a state-of-the-art facility. The library was placed at the heart of the campus, overlooking a secluded courtyard.

The enlarged library embraced this exterior space with five "pavilions" that projected into the courtyard. Each pavilion has windows on all four sides, including glass corners so that the students could feel as if they were in the garden. The interior of each pavilion was treated separately, with an identifying color of wall paint and carpet, each one lined with low maple bookcases. Sustainable materials were used throughout.

The fifth pavilion was the home of the faculty lounge, sitting at the helm of the entire plan and reflecting the teaching philosophy of Rudolph Steiner, the pedagogical basis of Waldorf schools, that the teaching material come directly from the educator—not from standard secondary-source textbooks.

WHAT WE DO   MILLER LIBRARY, WALDORF SCHOOL

1. ENTRY
2. CIRCULATION DESK
3. PRE-SCHOOL LIBRARY
4. MAIN LIBRARY SPACE
5. INDIVIDUAL READING ROOMS
6. FACULTY LOUNGE & CONFERENCE ROOM
7. FACULTY MAILBOXES
8. RECEPTION
9. FACULTY OFFICE
10. LIBRARIAN'S OFFICE

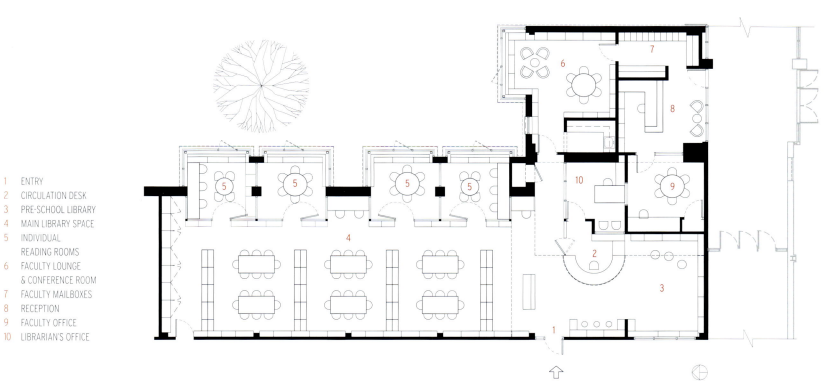

ROUGE TOMATE

New York, New York | 2008

At this Eastside Manhattan restaurant, an innovative food concept from Belgium was introduced to the U.S. The design was inspired by that of the original Rouge Tomate in Brussels and equally by its nutritional mission, *Sanitas Per Escam* or Health Through Food. This deep respect for ingredients and nutritionally balanced dishes was expressed in the design's spare geometries, natural materials, and discreet displays of foliage and fresh produce.

The space to be occupied presented both challenges and unusual opportunities. Comprising the street floor and basement of an imposing, circa 1900, commercial building, it offered generous interior volumes and tall windows along the street. Certain appealing elements of the store that had occupied the two floors were retained, notably the ample openings in the street floor, which allowed the two levels to be seen at once, and the dramatic stairs that linked them.

Entering patrons crossed a glass-railed bridge to reach the greeter station, emblazoned with red squares evoking Rouge Tomate's logo, set against a wall paneled with larger red squares. The centerpiece of the street-level lounge was a vivid red juice bar, its blenders in a glass enclosure to mute their sounds. In a similar position on the dining floor below, a screen of wood slats partially concealed the brightly lit display kitchen. A back-lighted wood slat wall, with niches displaying plants and produce, served as a backdrop for both floors.

An open walnut wood stair between the levels rose above a shallow pool with floating trays of cranberries, again repeating the four-by-four red squares of the restaurant's symbol. Two booths of seating cantilevered over the opening providing secluded nooks with broad views and two booths beneath nestled into the cranberry pool. Between the street-level windows, and extending down to the dining space below, were back-lighted photos on glass by artist Per Fronth, evoking a sunlit forest setting and simultaneously concealing wine racks and creating the sense of windows in the lower dining room.

CORRELATIONS: LIFE + WORK — BENTEL & BENTEL ARCHITECTS

1. ENTRY BRIDGE
2. GREETER
3. TWO-STORY ARTWORK & WINE RACK
4. TOMATO TOWER
5. JUICE ROOM
6. BAR
7. CASUAL DINING
8. DINING
9. BALCONY BOOTHS
10. WINE STORAGE
11. PENINSULA BOOTHS
12. PRIVATE DINING ROOM
13. CRANBERRY POOL
14. SERVICE AREA
15. DISPLAY KITCHEN
16. OPEN TO BELOW
C. COATS
T. TOILETS
KIT. KITCHEN

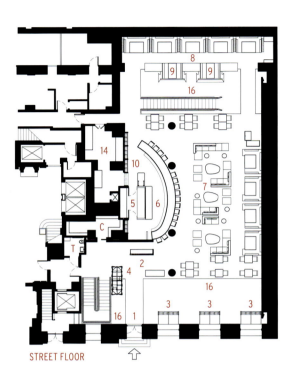

STREET FLOOR

PREVIOUS PAGES: Entry area with views of upper and lower dining levels
TOP (LEFT TO RIGHT): Lower-level dining; Stairway and booths cantilevered over cranberry pool; Upper-level juice bar
BELOW RIGHT: Lower-level dining, tomato tower, and display kitchen

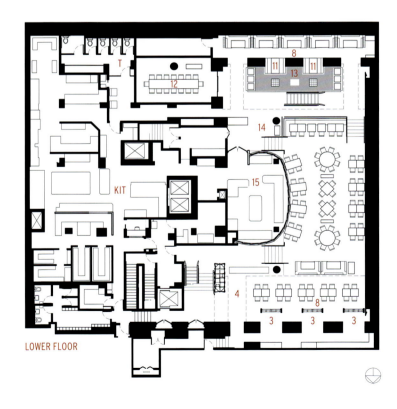

LOWER FLOOR

WHAT WE DO   ROUGE TOMATE

CORRELATIONS: LIFE + WORK   BENTEL & BENTEL ARCHITECTS

ABOVE (LEFT TO RIGHT): Balcony of One 80 suite; Living room view from kitchen
OPPOSITE: Bedroom suite
FOLLOWING PAGES: Living area

RED ROCK CASINO, VIP SUITES

Las Vegas, Nevada | 2008

The six penthouse suites atop the Red Rock Casino constitute the capstone of the resort complex. Laid out along a curved central corridor, they offer optimal views of the legendary Las Vegas Strip to the east and the extraordinary terrain of Red Rock Canyon to the west.

Each suite has a gently curving linear layout—allowing sweeping views from each of its component areas for living, dining, recreation, bathing, and sleeping—all supported by efficient service facilities and extensive audio-visual installations. Ceiling planes angling upward toward the tall glass exterior walls enhance the sense of spaciousness and the panoramic outlooks. Concealed lighting incorporated in the architectural detailing expertly illuminates the spaces. The master bathrooms feature island tubs clad, like the walls, in elegant marble slabs.

There are distinctions among the suites in the specifics of their layouts and the moods they set. The range of colors and textures of their surfaces and furnishings explore particular portions of the spectrum, such as off-whites and beiges, greens and earth tones, and a range of golds. Whatever their color themes, these interiors exhibit the inherent properties of their woods, stones, leathers, metals, fabrics, and carpets. And all of the interior treatments maintain a perceptual kinship with the natural formations of the celebrated landscape outside.

For the One 80 suite, at one end of the floor, with three exposures and a generous balcony, the architects assembled a dusky palette of wenge wood, Nero Marquina stone, blackened stainless steel, and metallic gunmetal gray leather. Weaving them together are sinuous glowing walls of low-iron sandblasted glass—intended to dissolve into and reflect the nocturnal desert outside. The architects identify this suite as "a celebration of the merry wanderers of the night for whom the day holds no mystery."

CORRELATIONS: LIFE + WORK   BENTEL & BENTEL ARCHITECTS

WHAT WE DO   RED ROCK CASINO, VIP SUITES

CORRELATIONS: LIFE + WORK   BENTEL & BENTEL ARCHITECTS

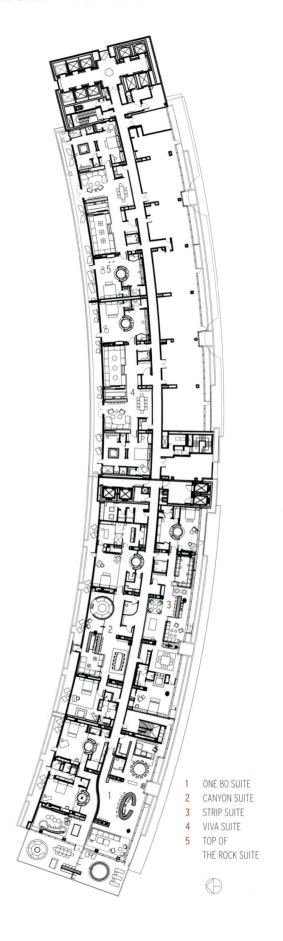

1 ONE 80 SUITE
2 CANYON SUITE
3 STRIP SUITE
4 VIVA SUITE
5 TOP OF
  THE ROCK SUITE

WHAT WE DO   RED ROCK CASINO, VIP SUITES

OPPOSITE (TOP TO BOTTOM): Canyon Suite living room;
Viva Suite bathroom; Viva Suite living area
RIGHT (CLOCKWISE FROM LEFT): One 80 Suite corridor; Balcony; Bar

CORRELATIONS: LIFE + WORK   BENTEL & BENTEL ARCHITECTS

 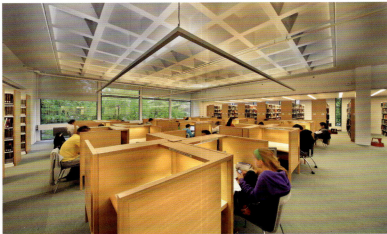

ABOVE (LEFT TO RIGHT): Building that houses library; Quiet Zone with custom-designed carrels
OPPOSITE: Reference desk

AXINN LIBRARY, HOFSTRA UNIVERSITY

Hempstead, New York | 2006

The renovation of the Axinn Library at Hofstra University transformed the worn and cluttered interior of a cast concrete structure, designed by Warner Burns Toan & Lunde. The result is a facility that offers students state-of-the-art comfort and technology, a variety of study venues, and easy access to books and staff. Decades of ill-considered modifications had encrusted the spaces with partitions, sprinkler pipes, and conduits that produced, in effect, a parking garage with haphazard insertions. Moreover, these intrusions had blocked appealing views through floor-to-ceiling windows of Hofstra's nationally recognized campus arboretum.

The firm's approach was to enhance the 1960s Brutalist architecture by scraping away accretions and overlaying new fluid and luminous elements to give the library a contemporary sense of welcome and comfort. The heaviness of the original concrete construction was offset with visually featherweight components: panels of frosted glass, mesh curtains, and suspended ceiling panels of reflective metal.

Sympathetic to the consistent gray of the exposed concrete were subtly contrasting colors ranging from white through ivory, along with polished stainless steel and warmer tones of wood. Softly diffused up-lighting made a visual virtue of the coffered concrete ceilings above the spaces.

The renovation carried out here focused exclusively on the library's first floor. The previously crowded array of circulation and reference departments, group and private study areas were effectively reorganized. A small café was added in a formerly under-used elevator lobby. Throughout, the rectangularity of the structural elements is echoed in a variety of lightweight and luminous elements, juxtaposed in certain areas with boldly curvilinear counters and seating. To carry out this rectangle-vs-curve theme appropriately in scale and detail, all tables, desks, and counters were designed by the architects. The resulting interiors effectively meet the library's updated academic and social needs while complementing the essential order of the original structure.

CORRELATIONS: LIFE + WORK   BENTEL & BENTEL ARCHITECTS

WHAT WE DO AXINN LIBRARY, HOFSTRA UNIVERSITY

CORRELATIONS: LIFE + WORK — BENTEL & BENTEL ARCHITECTS

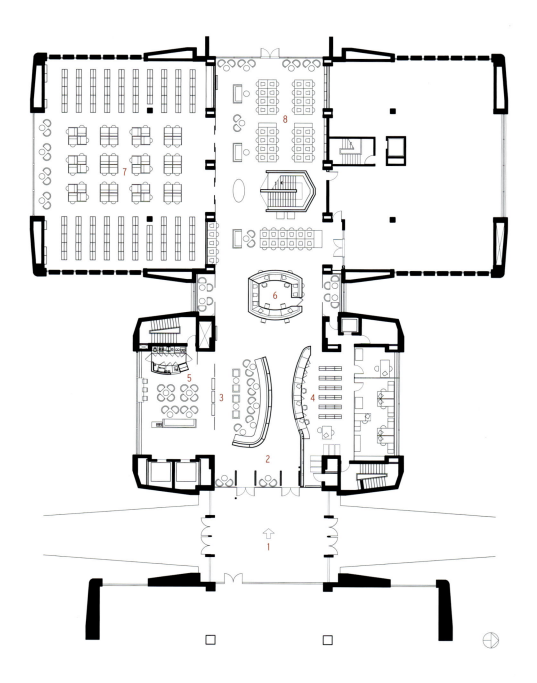

1. LOBBY
2. ENTRY
3. NEW BOOKS
4. CIRCULATION
5. CAFÉ
6. REFERENCE DESK
7. QUIET STUDY
8. COMPUTER CARRELS

WHAT WE DO   AXINN LIBRARY, HOFSTRA UNIVERSITY

PREVIOUS PAGES: Library seen from entrance
TOP TO BOTTOM: Looking into café with campus view; New book reading area

CORRELATIONS: LIFE + WORK — BENTEL & BENTEL ARCHITECTS

ABOVE (LEFT TO RIGHT): **Hotel in downtown setting; Entries at corner and along street front; Check-in seen from lounge**
OPPOSITE: **Lounge and bar seen from street**

W HOTEL, MARKET RESTAURANT, AND DESCENT BAR

Boston, Massachusetts | 2010

Accommodating 230 luxury hotel rooms and 111 condominium units, the twenty-six-story glass-clad hotel rose as a beacon for Boston's largely low-rise theater district. Bentel & Bentel designed the entire hotel interior and the Market restaurant (recently renamed the Gallery) for a prominent street-level space with its own entrance, and the lower-level Descent Bar.

Taking cues from the sleek building envelope, the interiors were treated as crisply modern, with materials of largely neutral color: stainless steel, natural woods, frosted glass, leather, and muted fabrics. The lobby and the restaurant are visible from the street through floor-to-ceiling glass and offer patrons behind it views of theater-related street activity. The lobby design responds to its public visibility with sheer curtains, cozy seating alcoves, and a reassuring gas-burning hearth. Its island bar was shaped to encourage conviviality.

Designed for the eminent chef Jean-Georges Vongerichten, the Market complements the hotel as a three-meal-a-day restaurant. Its design presents a contemporary interpretation of New England restraint and directness. Surfaces suggest the colors and textures of the seashore. A bleached oak canopy defines the central dining space visibly, from both the interior and the street. A bar at the far end of the space offers a secluded alternative to the lobby bar, serving light food as well as drinks.

Art figures prominently throughout the hotel's public spaces, guest rooms, and suites. The bedrooms feature wall-sized, translucent fabric panels depicting New England scenes, some quite literally, some highly abstract. On their bathroom sides, these panels offered nature-related quotes from the region's revered philosopher, Henry David Thoreau.

In sharp contrast to the high visibility of the hotel's public spaces, the architects designed the intimate basement-level Descent bar and lounge, subtly lighted and featuring curvilinear furnishings in shades of white and vivid red. Floating off-white ceiling and wall panels, arrayed irregularly, only partially conceal the rough concrete cavities behind them.

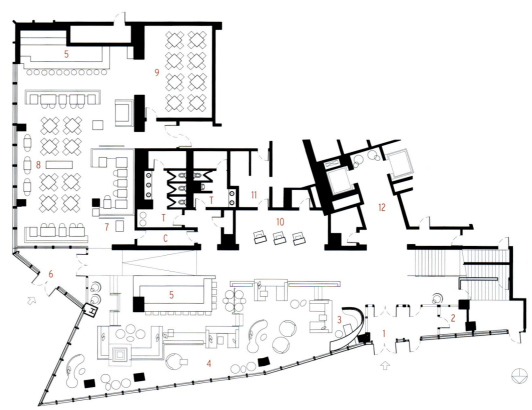

1   MAIN ENTRY
2   W STORE
3   CONCIERGE DESK
4   LOUNGE
5   BAR
6   THEATER DISTRICT ENTRY
7   MARKET RESTAURANT
8   DINING
9   PRIVATE DINING
10   CHECK-IN
11   OFFICES
12   ELEVATOR LOBBY
C   COATS
T   TOILETS

WHAT WE DO W HOTEL, MARKET RESTAURANT, AND DESCENT BAR

TOP LEFT: Concierge desk and Lounge
TOP TO BOTTOM: Lobby bar; Market restaurant

CORRELATIONS: LIFE + WORK BENTEL & BENTEL ARCHITECTS

WHAT WE DO   W HOTEL, MARKET RESTAURANT, AND DESCENT BAR

TOP (LEFT TO RIGHT): Guest room entry; "Welcome wall" with shelves and mirror; Bathroom with poem wall; Guest bedroom with translucent art wall
OPPOSITE BELOW: Another guest bedroom

1 W SUITE
2 DOUBLE ROOM
3 SINGLE KING ROOM
T TOILET

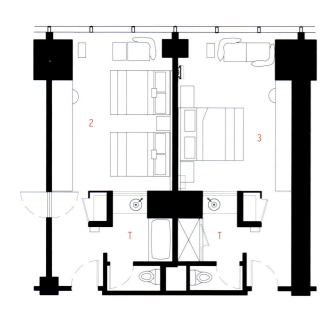
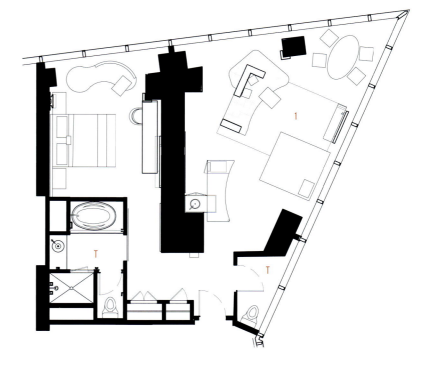

127

WHAT WE DO   W HOTEL, MARKET RESTAURANT, AND DESCENT BAR

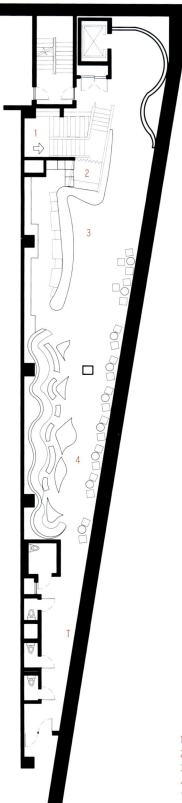

OPPOSITE (TOP TO BOTTOM): Descent Bar lounge seating; Descent Bar
ABOVE: Entry stair and DJ booth off landing

1 ENTRY
2 DJ BOOTH
3 BAR
4 LOUNGE
T TOILETS

CORRELATIONS: LIFE + WORK   BENTEL & BENTEL ARCHITECTS

LE BERNARDIN

New York, New York | 2011

The intention in redesigning this renowned four-star restaurant was to update the entire space, while enlarging the bar-lounge and making it a destination in itself. Chef Eric Ripert's words to describe his vision for it: "convivial, warm, sexy, serene."

The first design decision was to retain the iconic teak ceiling and upgrade the lighting within it to provide a pool of light for each table. Everything below the ceiling was completely redesigned.

The lounge area was made more welcoming by opening a new window overlooking the through-block walkway outside. The curved plan of its bar added to its conviviality and made it an appealing setting for the chef to prepare some plates there, within view of patrons. Low banquettes, with easily movable casual seats and tables, set an informal tone.

The screen that divided the dining room from the lounge brought the teak of the ceiling down into the occupied space in an assemblage of teak blocks, subtly lighted from below. The same kind of teak composition defined alcoves deeper into the dining room.

Views into and out of the restaurant were controlled with scrims made of dried vines and metallic threads. On the dining room's interior wall screens of vertical, twisted aluminum strips, backlit, make the space seem less confined. Banquettes and chairs designed by the architects contribute to the restaurant's comfort and distinction. Colors throughout are in a range of grays, tans, and browns associated with the seaside.

At the far end of the dining room, a wall-sized painting by Ran Ortner underscores the seaside theme with an image that is active yet relaxing. Unlike art commissioned for many Bentel & Bentel interiors, this painting was fortuitously found, just waiting for an ideal setting.

Le Bernardin received a James Beard Award for best restaurant design in 2012 and was named Number 1 Restaurant in the World by La Liste, 2018.

TOP (LEFT TO RIGHT): Greeter station; Screen of acoustic fabric and twisted aluminum strips; Casual dining and bar
BELOW RIGHT: Main dining room with backdrop of Ran Ortner painting

WHAT WE DO   LE BERNARDIN

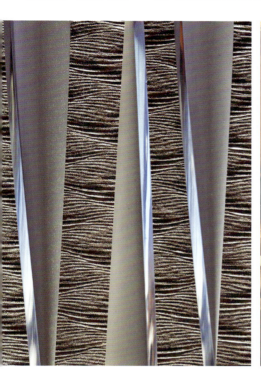

CORRELATIONS: LIFE + WORK   BENTEL & BENTEL ARCHITECTS

WHAT WE DO   LE BERNARDIN

CORRELATIONS: LIFE + WORK   BENTEL & BENTEL ARCHITECTS

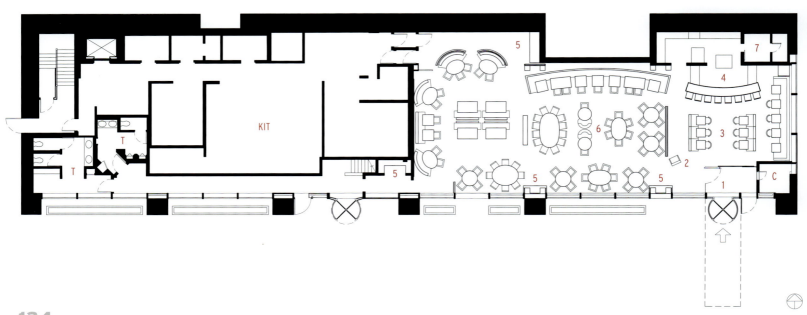

134

WHAT WE DO   LE BERNARDIN

PREVIOUS PAGES: Main dining room beyond teak screen
OPPOSITE: Booths backed by teak screens
ABOVE: Main dining room window wall

1 ENTRY
2 GREETER
3 CASUAL DINING
4 BAR
5 GUERIDON
6 DINING
7 WINE ROOM
T TOILETS
C COATS
KIT KITCHEN

135

CORRELATIONS: LIFE + WORK   BENTEL & BENTEL ARCHITECTS

APELLA AND RIVERPARK

New York, New York | 2011

TOP (LEFT TO RIGHT): **Apella conference center entry and reception; Conference room**
BELOW RIGHT: **Lounge with East River view**

For the campus of the East River Science Park, with its sweeping water views, the firm designed the state-of-the-art Apella conference center and—integrated with it—the Riverpark restaurant. The interior architecture of both was inspired by their waterfront site and the clean detailing of the high-rise in which they are located. Design features of both make reference to the ancient lighthouse at Pharos—the symbol of Alexandria Real Estate, the site's developer.

The conference center, reached by a spiral stair from the building lobby, expresses the presence of light as a concept with a consistent palette of glossy-white ceilings, translucent glass walls, buff travertine floors, and slots of lighting separating surface planes. Unusual materials support the lighthouse metaphor: a reception area wall displaying nineteenth-century lighthouse lens technology; glowing corridor walls with thin slices of open-cell foamed aluminum behind sheets of clear glass; oxidized steel walls pierced by hexagonal prisms originally devised to direct light through ship decks down to cargo holds.

Riverpark restaurant was designed to serve both as an urban amenity, available to all, and as a key component of the science park. With generous river views, it enjoys ample daylight from three directions. The main dining area is centered on a platform under an illuminated trellis, which extends over the bar. Dining areas directly overlooking the East River are under a textured bronze ceiling panel depicting the river's flow. The spare modern detailing of the overall space was here executed in a rich palette of white oak, French limestone, bronze, and frosted glass.

Two private dining spaces to the south of the main restaurant were scaled to meet the varied spatial demands of business meetings, conferences, and related dining, the larger of them divisible to serve two events simultaneously. Glass partitions with translucent artworks composed of scientific symbols, entitled *Clouds*, by Dutch graphic designer Karel Martens, open to expand the restaurant to the private dining areas.

WHAT WE DO   APELLA AND RIVERPARK

OPPOSITE: Apella breakout space
TOP: Corridor

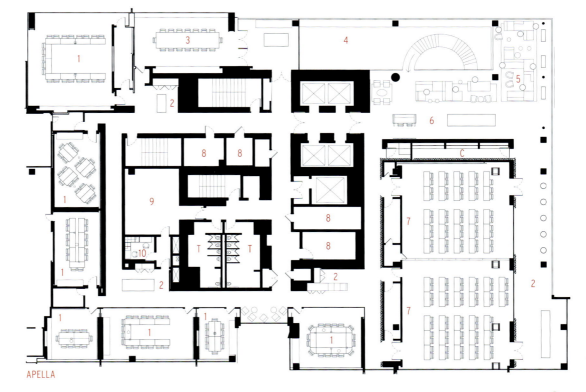

1 CONFERENCE ROOM
2 BREAKOUT SPACE
3 BOARD ROOM
4 OPEN TO BELOW
5 LOUNGE
6 RECEPTION
7 AUDITORIUM
8 STORAGE
9 PANTRY
10 OFFICE
C COATS

CORRELATIONS: LIFE + WORK BENTEL & BENTEL ARCHITECTS

WHAT WE DO APELLA AND RIVERPARK

TOP (LEFT TO RIGHT): Riverpark restaurant, dining platform under bronze trellis; Entry view; Detail of *Clouds* pattern by Karel Martens on translucent movable partition; Closer detail of *Clouds*
BELOW LEFT: Bar and tables overlooking East River
FOLLOWING PAGES: Main dining room, with movable partitions open to private dining room beyond

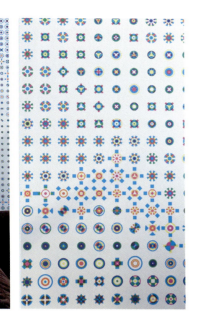

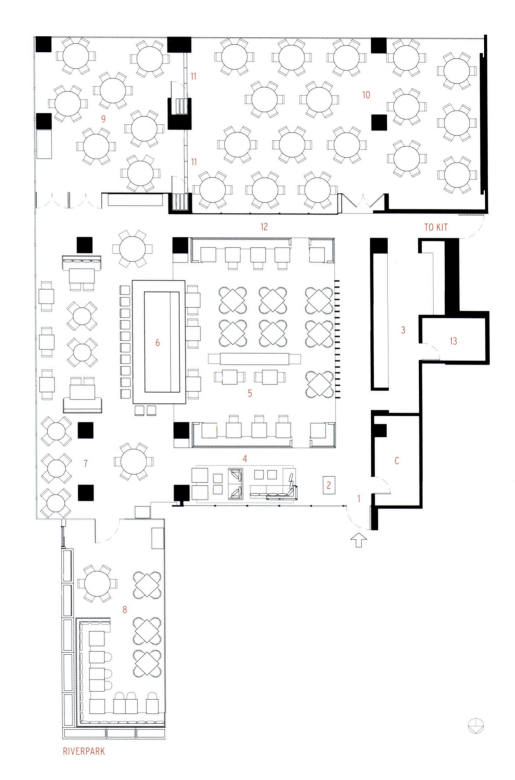

1 ENTRY
2 GREETER
3 BEVERAGE/SERVICE
4 WAITING
5 DINING PLATFORM
6 BAR
7 DINING
8 OUTDOOR DINING
9 SMALL PRIVATE DINING ROOM
10 LARGE PRIVATE DINING ROOM
11 SLIDING PARTITION
12 SLIDING ART WALL
13 OFFICE
C COATS
KIT KITCHEN

RIVERPARK

141

CORRELATIONS: LIFE + WORK   BENTEL & BENTEL ARCHITECTS

 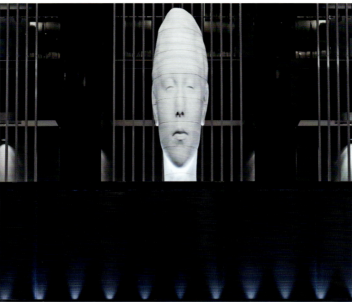

TOP (LEFT TO RIGHT): **Front of hotel with Chrysler Building beyond; Sculpture above fountain**
OPPOSITE: **Entry and lobby with fountain and sculptures by Jaume Plensa**

GRAND HYATT HOTEL

New York, New York | 2010

The mission here was to renew the public spaces of a 1,300-room hotel in the heart of Manhattan, on 42nd Street adjoining Grand Central Terminal. The vast main lobby was reconceived as an indoor urban space, guiding patrons entering at several points, serving them with registration and concierge facilities and generous seating, while directing them to elevators, meeting rooms, and a variety of food and beverage offerings. The necessity of rising two levels from 42nd Street was eased with the welcome of a cascading fountain inside the main entrance and a discreetly placed two-level elevator.

The colors of the space were transformed from assertive reds and golds to tranquil whites and blues under muted, expertly directed lighting. The up-lighting of the ceiling was programmed to change over 24 hours, with warmer tones at the hours of sunrise and sunset. Urban-scaled sculptures *Awilda* and *Chloe* by Jaume Plensa underlined the indoor piazza concept.

A twenty-four-hour Market adjoins the lobby through a blackened steel proscenium. Lighting of its upbeat interior includes internally illuminated columns and other sources focused on food offerings. The meeting room suite incorporates a pre-function room with casual seating and a service counter, two wood-and-glass "pavilions," and a central "studio" dining area. Movable walls allowed these spaces to be assigned separately or variously combined. The corridor adjoining all of the rooms is lined with a painting series, entitled *Walking Horizons*, by Burghard Müller-Dannhausen, visible from inside each glass pavilion.

A new restaurant takes maximum advantage of existing space projecting above the hotel's 42nd Street entrance. With both its walls and roof of clear glass, it offers a unique river-to-river view across Midtown Manhattan. Horizontal louvers within it deflect direct sunlight. A new granite stair and elevator provide access from the main lobby. The bar, lounge, and dining areas of the linear space are unified by a 100-foot-long suspended sculpture composed of stainless-steel tubes with integral lighting. This sculptural assemblage is purposely visible from the street, along with the internally illuminated bar, identifying the restaurant for passersby below.

CORRELATIONS: LIFE + WORK BENTEL & BENTEL ARCHITECTS

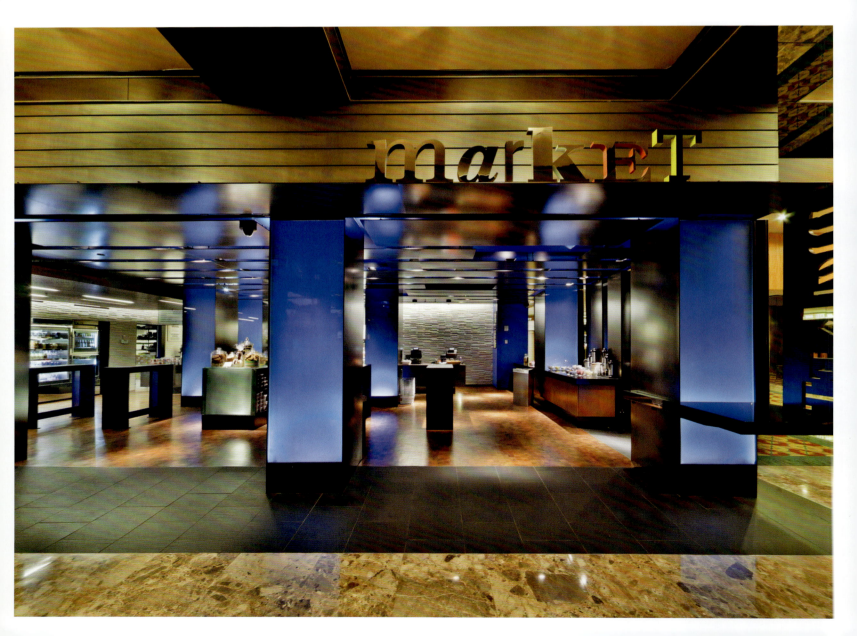

WHAT WE DO GRAND HYATT HOTEL

TOP (LEFT TO RIGHT): New York Central lounge; Bar under assembly of stainless-steel lighting tubes; Lighted bar; Galleries at Lex breakout areas; Breakout area with *Walking Horizons* painting by Burghard Müller-Dannhausen
BELOW LEFT: Market shop

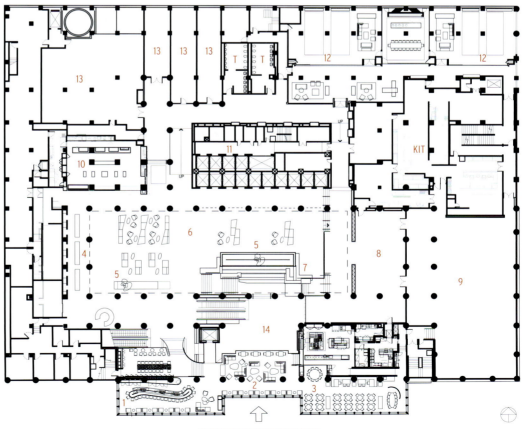

1 NEW YORK CENTRAL RESTAURANT BAR
2 LOUNGE
3 NEW YORK CENTRAL RESTAURANT
4 CHECK-IN DESK
5 SCULPTURE
6 LOBBY LOUNGE
7 FOUNTAIN
8 BALLROOM ENTRY
9 BALLROOM
10 MARKET
11 SERVICE
12 GALLERIES AT LEX CONFERENCE SPACES
13 SHOPS
14 LOBBY AT STREET LEVEL ENTRY
T TOILETS
KIT KITCHEN

ENTRY BELOW AT STREET LEVEL

147

WHAT WE DO   GROUND CAFÉ, YALE UNIVERSITY

OPPOSITE: Café and digital canvas
TOP Views of café from outside

GROUND CAFÉ, YALE UNIVERSITY
New Haven, Connecticut | 2012

Located in the Becton Center at Yale's School of Engineering and Applied Sciences, the Ground Café was intended to encourage social contact, not only among that school's faculty and students, but with the many others who pass it daily along a busy pedestrian route. The café's design was a sensitive response to its architectural setting, a building designed by the esteemed architect Marcel Breuer and completed in 1970, which embodies his characteristic sculptural creativity with exposed concrete.

Adapting a former seminar room on the building's street floor, the architects expanded it by a third of its original area. The room's aluminum-framed glass wall, which had been tucked well behind the building's bold structural frame, was replicated in an extension that gives the café visibility from the street, while still being sheltered under the overhang of the building's upper floors.

Inside the café, the architects made a point of exposing much of the rough-textured concrete of the building's interior. But they gave the space a warmer, more intimate quality—and improved its acoustics—by superimposing compositions of walnut staves and perforated aluminum sheets on walls and ceiling. To extend the floor of the original room into the extension, variegated bluestone was acquired from its flooring's original quarry and applied as well to one wall as a wainscot material.

In a bolder move to give the café an identity akin to its technology-related setting, they installed an LED digital "canvas," covering much of the ceiling and one wall. The images projected on this surface can display work by the researchers occupying this building or by students and faculty of Yale's other schools. Visible to all who visit or pass by, these digital displays serve to reinforce links between this school and the rest of Yale.

WHAT WE DO GROUND CAFÉ, YALE UNIVERSITY

OPPOSITE (TOP TO BOTTOM): Café and service counter; Walls of walnut staves
RIGHT (LEFT TO RIGHT): Detail of "canvas" for digital display; Detail of wall

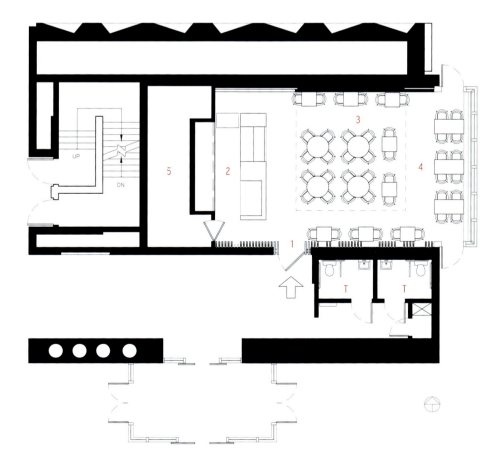

1 ENTRY
2 SERVICE COUNTER
3 CAFÉ SEATING
4 DIGITAL ARRAY AT WALL AND CEILING ABOVE
5 PANTRY
T TOILETS

151

HYATT REGENCY

Chicago, Illinois | 2013

TOP (LEFT TO RIGHT): Entrance canopy seen from street; Gardened exterior seating area; Entry to lobby with fountain and *River* sculpture by Ben Butler
BELOW RIGHT: Under entrance canopy

Located along the Chicago River, at the very crossroads of the city, the hotel is both an urban landmark and a flag-bearer for an international brand. And within it, such public amenities as the Big Bar and Stetson's restaurant are landmarks in themselves.

Bentel & Bentel's twenty-first-century renovations of the hotel responded to evolving guest expectations and to developments nearby, including the transformative Riverwalk right out front and the nearby Millennium Park. Their design interventions start at the main automobile entrance, with new paving that directs people to the entry doors. A new glazed vestibule brings visitors to the point where their internal paths are clearly visible.

The hotel's spacious skylit atrium, with its two levels of services and amenities, needed more than refurbishing. A major rearrangement of its components yielded clear paths of movement for guests and the public to their objectives—and more congenial settings for their activities.

Thorough redesign of the atrium included removal of a large pool occupying much of the entry level and introducing a raised, linear "river" that serves to direct visitors along a major axis. A graceful new stair to the second level artfully obscures the view of starkly functional escalator banks. Painting the atrium roof frame dark blue minimized its presence and the apparent steel bulk, under which wood-like beams were attached to add warmth. Dividing the first-level dining areas into smaller spaces under trellises provided a desired intimacy. The route to the well-known Stetson's restaurant was made more apparent both inside and out, and the addition of windows yielded a more appealing image from adjoining streets.

On the second level, the traditional forbidding desk was replaced by individual tear-shaped counters. The Big Bar there was enlarged, with a 100-foot-long video display that doesn't block its expansive view over the river. Custom bar stools and a wavy "river" carpet designed by the architects enhance the area. And a clutter of bottles there was replaced with a memorable glowing liquor tower.

WHAT WE DO   HYATT REGENCY

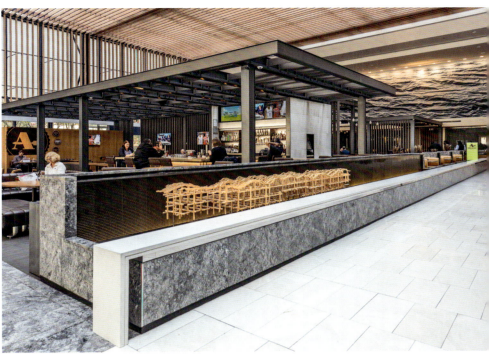
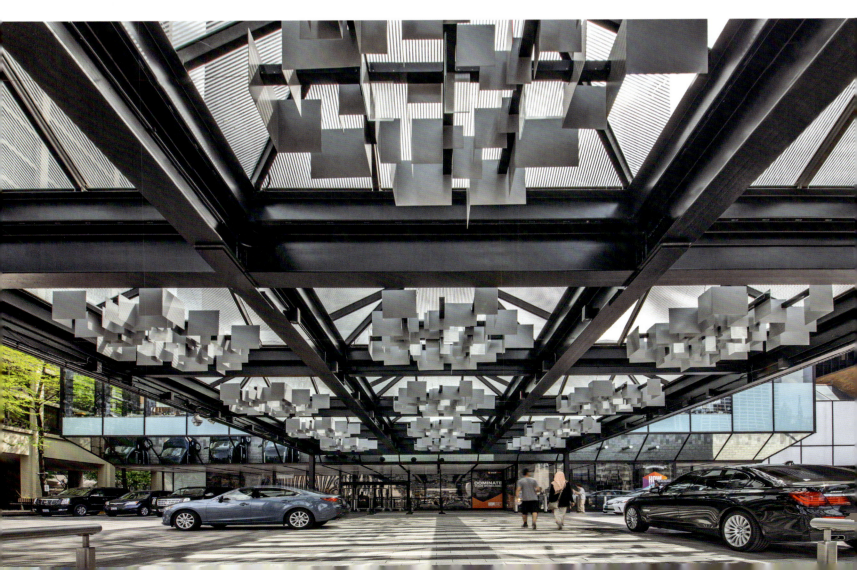

TOP TO BOTTOM: Market coffee shop; Check-in area on mezzanine
OPPOSITE: Main dining and lounge area seen from mezzanine

CORRELATIONS: LIFE + WORK   BENTEL & BENTEL ARCHITECTS

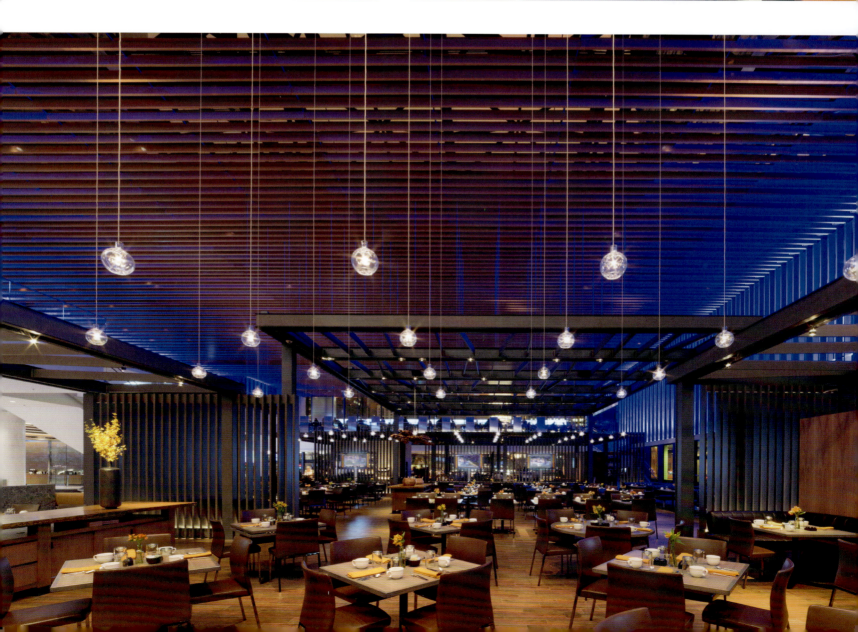

WHAT WE DO HYATT REGENCY

TOP (LEFT TO RIGHT): **Stetson's Steakhouse**; **Private dining room with sculpture by Ben Butler**; **Mural of Lake Michigan by Ben Butler**
BELOW LEFT: **3-Meal restaurant**
FOLLOWING PAGES: **Big Bar**, where televisions and city views can both be enjoyed

1 ENTRY
2 ENTRY CANOPY
3 EXTERIOR SEATING
4 LOUNGE
5 BAR
6 3-MEAL RESTAURANT
7 PRIVATE DINING
8 BUFFET
9 STETSON'S STEAKHOUSE
10 MARKET COFFEE SHOP
11 FOUNTAIN
12 BANQUET ROOMS
T TOILETS
KIT KITCHEN

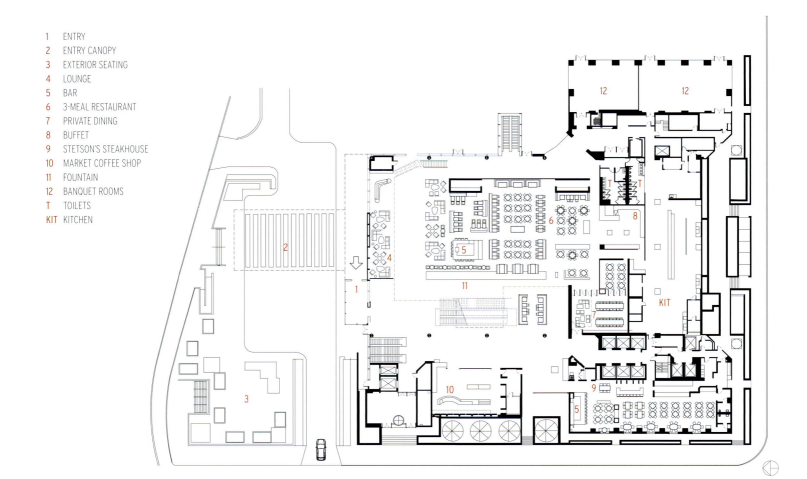

CORRELATIONS: LIFE + WORK BENTEL & BENTEL ARCHITECTS

WHAT WE DO HYATT REGENCY

CORRELATIONS: LIFE + WORK — BENTEL & BENTEL ARCHITECTS

RENWICK GALLERY

Renwick Gallery Grand Salon Design Competition | 2013

The Renwick Gallery in Washington is both a national museum of contemporary design and craft and a well-preserved architectural landmark, built in the 1860s in the Second Empire style. Created to house the extraordinary Corcoran collection, it served a variety of purposes when that institution moved to new, larger quarters nearby and was saved from destruction in 1962 for its present use and named for its renowned architect, James Renwick, Jr.

The Grand Salon is the Renwick's central, large-scaled gallery, reached by an axial grand stair from the entrance area and evoking the splendor of nineteenth-century Paris. In 2013, the museum mounted an invited architectural competition for a treatment of this great room reflecting both its Classical inspiration and its role in the celebration of contemporary design.

As their competition entry, Bentel & Bentel proposed a design to envelope the viewer while leaving the existing interior visible. It would have been simultaneously a sculptural object in itself, a veil or scrim through which the existing enclosure remained visible, and a source of varying, programmable light and sound. The intriguing variability of the experience was expected to encourage return visits.

The complex geometry of the firm's proposed construction has distinct but interacting sources: a network of diagonals and a set of overlapping circles in plan; a series of parabolic curves in section. The three-dimensional results were to be domelike lattices, three of them intersecting within the salon, a fourth over the stairs.

Construction would have been of preformed metal tubes, transferring all structural loads to floor level and carrying power for LED lighting along the tubes, with point sources at intersections. When the tracery was illuminated, it would have occupied the foreground. With the surfaces behind it illuminated, the emphasis would have been on the historic architecture.

TOP (LEFT TO RIGHT): Entry via stair; Main space; Main space in lecture format
BELOW: 3D drawing

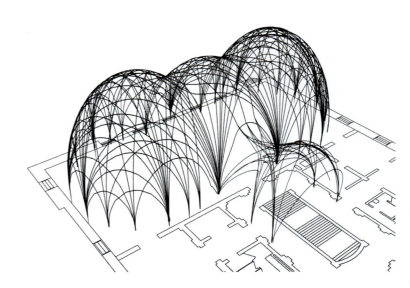

WHAT WE DO RENWICK GALLERY

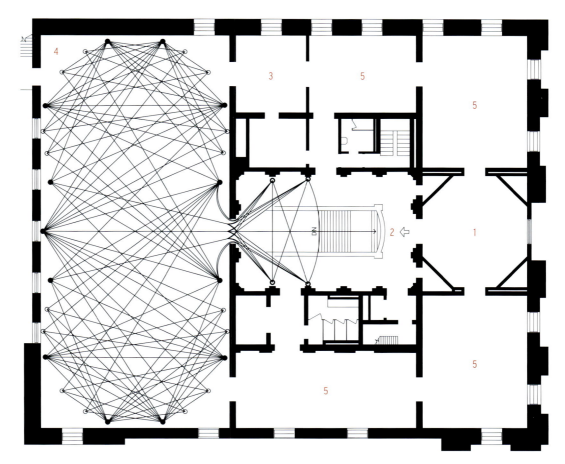

1. OCTAGON ROOM
2. STAIR COURT
3. MEDIA ROOM
4. GRAND SALON
5. GALLERY (EXISTING)

CORRELATIONS: LIFE + WORK   BENTEL & BENTEL ARCHITECTS

TOP (LEFT TO RIGHT): Former carriage houses occupied by restaurant; Entry and view into bar room; Dining room with planter light; Communal table in bar room
BELOW RIGHT: Dining room and open kitchen

ROUGE TOMATE CHELSEA

New York, New York | 2016

Relocated to the Chelsea area of Manhattan, Rouge Tomate was designed to occupy a pair of former carriage houses dating from 1864. Designated city landmarks, the paired structures had most recently served as a truck garage. Given Rouge Tomate's international mission to support the well-being of individual diners and the environment, this property in need of restoration was an ideal match.

The wine bar and restaurant were accommodated in two long spaces stretching back from the street front. The entrance and bar room shared one of these narrow volumes, separated by a clear glass wall. Reached from the bar room through a portal in a brick wall was the more spacious dining room, which seated seventy-five, with an unobstructed view of the kitchen to the rear. A private dining room seating thirty-two was on the second floor, accessible from the entrance area by a newly installed elevator.

In the entrance and bar areas, the illusion of an outdoor setting was established with a garden gate, stone paving, and backlit ceiling images of foliage, complemented by living vines. In the bar space, a stone wine vessel represented the age-old wine-making process. Reclaimed boards and end-grain wood blocks on the walls, along with live-edge wood tables, immersed patrons in the qualities of natural materials. A bronze bar top and custom-designed leather seating reinforced this theme and nodded toward the former carriage house use. The oak floor of the dining room displayed the natural curvature of the source trees.

On the restaurant's front, the large openings that once admitted carriages, then trucks, were filled in with low-glare glass to appear glassless. Folding doors flanking these openings replicated those in old photos. The colors of the repainted front recalled the red and green of Rouge Tomate's graphics and gained Landmarks Preservation Commission approval for these historical exteriors.

The restaurant won a 2017 New York State Preservation League Excellence Award.

WHAT WE DO ROUGE TOMATE CHELSEA

CORRELATIONS: LIFE + WORK BENTEL & BENTEL ARCHITECTS

TOP (LEFT TO RIGHT): Vestibule with ceiling of back-lighted foliage photos; Entry with view into bar room; Bar with wine room beyond
OPPOSITE: Dining counter at open kitchen

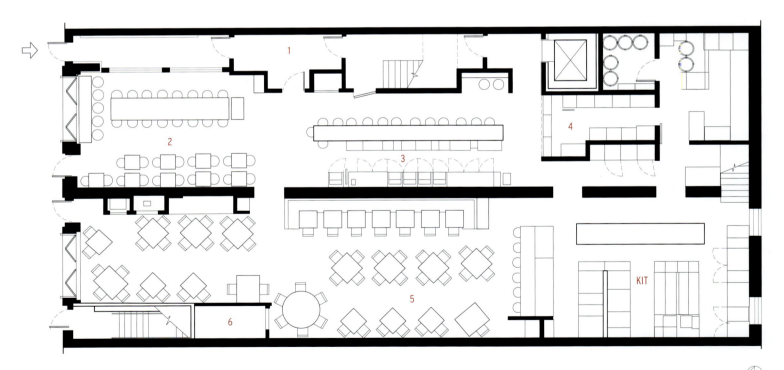

1 ENTRY
2 CASUAL DINING
3 BAR
4 WINE ROOM
5 DINING ROOM
6 CLOSET
KIT KITCHEN

WHAT WE DO   CLUB 432

OPPOSITE: **Entry corridor from elevator** ABOVE (LEFT TO RIGHT): **Entrance to wine room from lounge**; **Custom lounge chandelier**; **Entire lounge**

CLUB 432

New York, New York | 2017

For the 432 Park Avenue apartment tower that instantly remade the Manhattan skyline, developer Harry Macklowe commissioned Bentel & Bentel to design a suite of amenities for residents. Occupying the tower's entire 7,500-square-foot twelfth floor and opening onto 5,000 square feet of roof terrace, the facility comprises a full-service dining space and an equally large multipurpose lounge to provide for such functions as cocktail and tea service, performances, ceremonies, or just casual socializing.

The grand proportions of these two principal spaces—each twenty-five feet high and twenty-two feet six inches by eighty feet in floor area, with massive structural members framing ten-foot-square areas of glass—offered exceptional design opportunities. Yet they had to accommodate activities that often called for a more-intimate atmosphere.

Among the components that deal most effectively with this spatial challenge are a variety of suspended lighting installations. In the dining space, an array of hanging fixtures establishes a lower porous ceiling plane at twelve feet, six inches, more in keeping with anticipated parties of diners. In the lounge area two very tall lead crystal chandeliers, designed by the architects with Czech fabricators, reach down to more familiar heights. They can also imply the existence of two functionally distinct spaces within this palatial volume.

Throughout these spaces, the architects treated surfaces to resonate with the rectangular geometries and neutral color palette established in Rafael Viñoly's design of the tower itself. Stepping off an elevator, one enters a central corridor with marble flooring in a bold black-and-white geometrical pattern and walls of polished stainless steel and translucent glass. In the dining and lounge areas, carpets echo the geometries of the corridor floor in subtle shades of beige and gray. On the walls and ceilings of these principal volumes, a variety of uncoated materials—bleached and light-stained oak, mirrored glass, pale brown suede—are applied in rectangular configurations.

CORRELATIONS: LIFE + WORK BENTEL & BENTEL ARCHITECTS

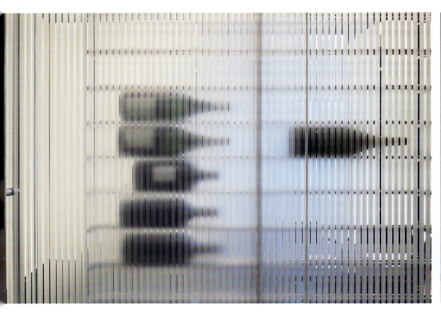

TOP (LEFT TO RIGHT): Wine room wall; Dining room
OPPOSITE: Lighting canopy above dining room counter

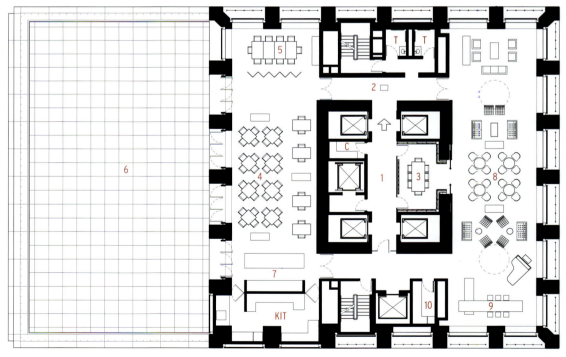

1 ENTRY
2 GREETER
3 WINE ROOM
4 DINING
5 PRIVATE DINING ROOM
6 OUTDOOR TERRACE
7 DISPLAY KITCHEN
8 LOUNGE
9 BAR
10 BEVERAGE/SERVICE
T TOILETS
C COATS
KIT KITCHEN

CORRELATIONS: LIFE + WORK   BENTEL & BENTEL ARCHITECTS

41 LINSKEY WAY

Cambridge, Massachusetts | 2017

For a former industrial area evolving into a district of tech enterprises, this design would expand and transform a small yet dignified former maple sugar canning factory, incorporating it visibly into a repurposed structure. The additions emulate the forthrightness of the original building's form and details. Materials of the added construction—granite, weathered wood and metal, board-formed concrete—are meant to age as gracefully as those of the core structure. The design purposely retains exterior views of the existing structure.

Design of the new exterior took further cues from the existing one. For instance, the broad door and window openings of the existing street-floor restaurant would be picked up in floor-to-ceiling glass on two street fronts. The regular rhythm of smaller openings on the existing building's second and third floors would be reflected in the pattern of weathered wood fins on much of the exterior. The rhythm and spacing of the existing brick piers would be recalled in the verticals framing the windows on all sides. Sheltered outdoor terraces would be provided on several floors.

As a means of binding the entire resulting structure together, a weathering metal wall rises from a dark granite base along one long exposed side. It would set out from the existing wall to accommodate new stairways for patrons and staff between the new metal skin and the existing brick façade. The landings of these new stairs would be enclosed with full-height glass, allowing unimpeded views of the original walls and the urban context beyond.

The primary use of the building would be as a private social and meeting place for members and their guests, with lounges, bar and dining facilities, and meeting rooms of various sizes. A first-floor restaurant would be open to the public, as would—seasonally—a rooftop bar.

LEFT TO RIGHT: **Entrance adjoining existing portion; Building in redeveloped area**

1   ENTRY
2   RECEPTION
3   CAFÉ
4   RESTAURANT
5   MEETING ROOM
6   AUDITORIUM
7   BAR
8   DINING/MEETING ROOM
9   STORAGE
10 PANTRY
T   TOILET
KIT KITCHEN

WHAT WE DO 41 LINSKEY WAY

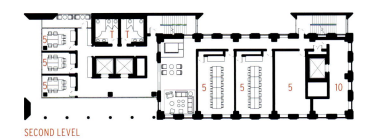
SECOND LEVEL

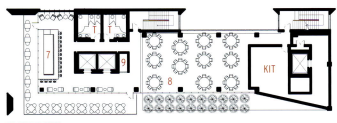
FOURTH LEVEL

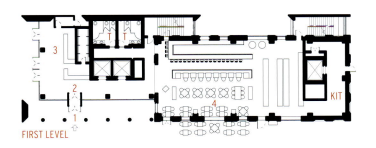
FIRST LEVEL

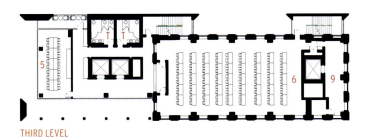
THIRD LEVEL

COUCH ACADEMIC CENTER, WEBB INSTITUTE

Glen Cove, New York | 2020

A naval architecture college housed in a 1912 mansion on a historic campus on Long Island Sound needed to expand. Before this addition, the students' classrooms had been located in the mansion along with their dorm rooms. The design task was to add 30,000 square feet of teaching space without destroying the view of and from the mansion or overwhelming its prominence on the site.

The firm's concept was to create a "non-building" hidden under a grassy terrace facing the Sound, offering the students broad views to the water and passing vessels as a connection to their naval studies. The new construction topped by a planted roof preserved the campus landscape while providing the students a lesson on environmental responsibility.

Inside, the building consists of state-of-the-art classrooms with space for both design and lecture classes and a joint space for all four years of students to mingle. Four double-size classrooms embrace an exterior courtyard, which could serve as an additional teaching space or accommodate special gatherings. Surrounding this courtyard are arcades that shield the classrooms from direct sunlight and solar heat gain.

The hallway that connects the two sets of classrooms, which students pass through daily, leads them along a historic brick wall with four ornamental niches that were part of the mansion's original garden terrace. A new tunnel, in the spirit of tunnels that already existed under the campus, connects the new building underground to the historic mansion.

The lower floor of the addition was designed to house a computer lab, a maker space, IT offices, and faculty offices. The existing academic space in the mansion was converted to additional dormitory space for women, who were previously housed in other campus buildings. The goals of providing expanded academic space and improving student housing were well accomplished, without harm to this exceptional historic property.

The Couch Academic Center was awarded Preservation Long Island's 2022 Preservation Award.

CORRELATIONS: LIFE + WORK   BENTEL & BENTEL ARCHITECTS

PREVIOUS PAGES: Central arcade seen from courtyard
TOP (LEFT TO RIGHT): Courtyard with Long Island Sound view; Arcade; Central lounge
BELOW: Core of campus with addition in foreground

WHAT WE DO COUCH ACADEMIC CENTER, WEBB INSTITUTE

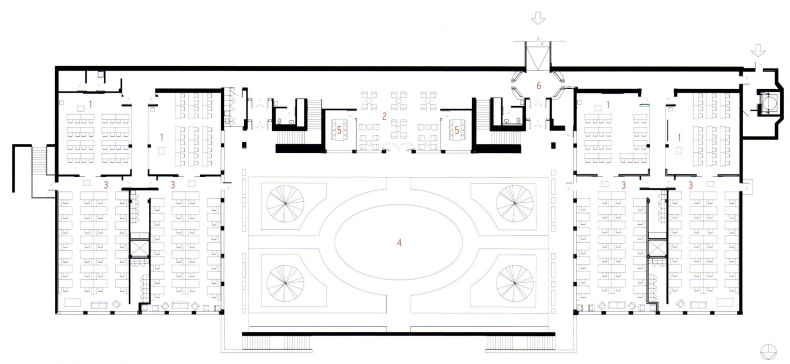

1 LECTURE ROOM
2 LOUNGE
3 CLASSROOM
4 COURTYARD
5 CONFERENCE ROOM
6 TUNNEL TO MAIN BUILDING

CORRELATIONS: LIFE + WORK   BENTEL & BENTEL ARCHITECTS

PALMS CASINO RESORT

Las Vegas, Nevada | 2019

TOP (LEFT TO RIGHT): **Palms Suite 1108C4 bar and games area; Bedroom**

The six Sky Villas at the top of the Palms Resort were designed with a particular clientele in mind: guests who are widely exposed to global influences and likely to be more knowledgeable about the arts than previous generations of "high rollers." When they seek luxury and share it with their friends, they bring greater appreciation for quality, craftsmanship, and exceptional amenities.

In shaping the suites, the architects maintained their established minimal design language to support a sense of more than ample space. Within that vocabulary the villas were given six unique identities through their individual material palettes, from the exuberant, orange-veined rainbow onyx, cerused oak, and polished steel of one villa to the regal, purple-striped Brescia Capraia marble, bleached walnut, and intense pale greens of another.

For the extraordinary Empathy Suite the resort's owners, who are major art collectors, proposed that the architects collaborate with the world-famous artist Damien Hirst. Among his six large-scale original artworks installed in the suite, his *Winner/Loser*—two bull sharks suspended in a tank of formaldehyde—greets the guests upon entry. Beyond individual works, his distinctive imagery has been incorporated into custom-designed furniture and appears on various surfaces as "tattoos" of signature Hirst motifs such as butterflies, diamond shapes, pills, and skulls. The prevailing material palette to set off these visual adventures is neutral in color but luxurious in detail—including richly white-veined gray marble, bleached white oak, frosted water-clear glass, cream white leather, and polished stainless steel.

At the center of the suite is a double-height space opening to an extensive balcony centered on a swimming pool that cantilevers out from the structure. Around that main space on the entry level are areas for dining, games, and media/theater. On the level above are two spacious bedroom zones, each extending out to offer occupants extensive views in three directions.

WHAT WE DO   PALMS CASINO RESORT

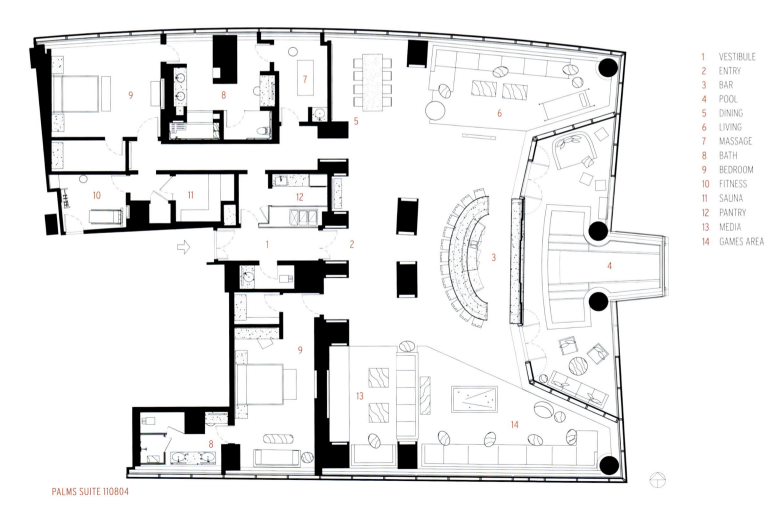

PALMS SUITE 110804

1	VESTIBULE
2	ENTRY
3	BAR
4	POOL
5	DINING
6	LIVING
7	MASSAGE
8	BATH
9	BEDROOM
10	FITNESS
11	SAUNA
12	PANTRY
13	MEDIA
14	GAMES AREA

CORRELATIONS: LIFE + WORK — BENTEL & BENTEL ARCHITECTS

WHAT WE DO PALMS CASINO RESORT

OPPOSITE (TOP TO BOTTOM): Palms Suite 110802 pool; Living room and bar
TOP: Bathroom

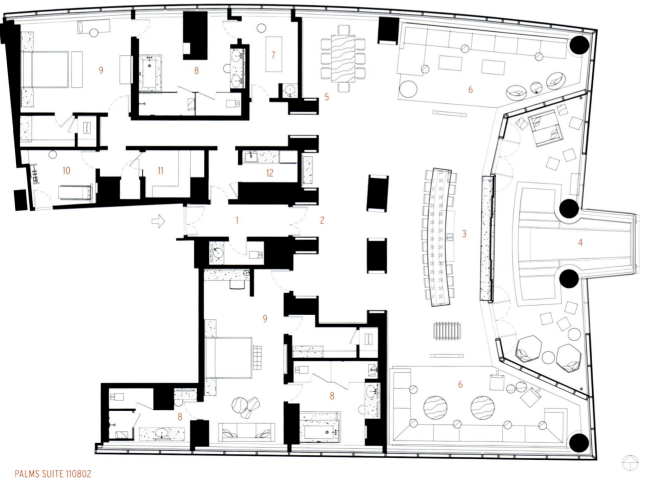

1	VESTIBULE
2	ENTRY
3	BAR
4	POOL
5	DINING
6	LIVING
7	MASSAGE
8	BATH
9	BEDROOM
10	FITNESS
11	SAUNA
12	PANTRY

PALMS SUITE 110802

CORRELATIONS: LIFE + WORK   BENTEL & BENTEL ARCHITECTS

TOP (LEFT TO RIGHT): Palms Suite 110805 view toward media room and stair; Bedroom; Bathroom

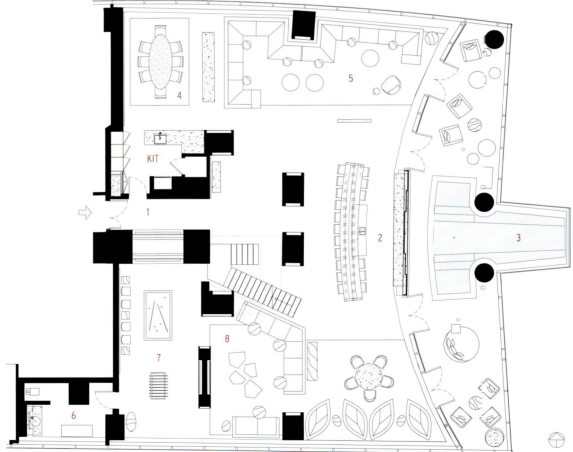

1 FOYER
2 BAR
3 POOL
4 DINING
5 LIVING
6 POWDER ROOM
7 GAMES
8 MEDIA
KIT KITCHEN

PALMS SUITE 110805 LOWER

WHAT WE DO   PALMS CASINO RESORT

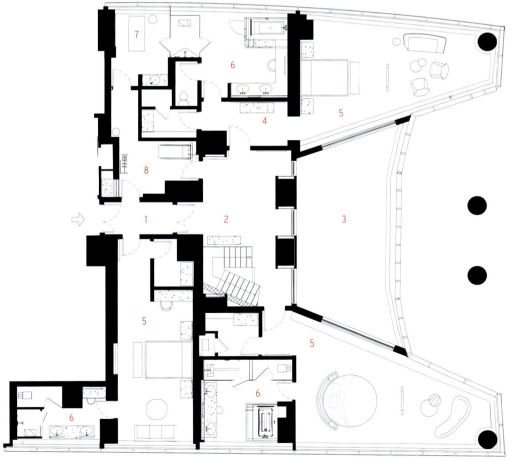

PALMS SUITE 110805 UPPER

1 VESTIBULE
2 STAIRHALL
3 OPEN TO BELOW
4 BEDROOM FOYER
5 BEDROOM
6 BATH
7 MASSAGE
8 FITNESS

CORRELATIONS: LIFE + WORK   BENTEL & BENTEL ARCHITECTS

LEFT: Empathy Suite bathroom
BELOW: Empathy Suite bedroom
OPPOSITE: Empathy Suite bar with Damien Hirst artworks above it

CORRELATIONS: LIFE + WORK **BENTEL & BENTEL ARCHITECTS**

HALL ARTS HOTEL

Dallas, Texas | 2019

The hotel was conceived as an integral component of the Dallas Arts District, the city's celebrated constellation of museums and performance halls. It occupies a ten-story building, part of a new complex that includes a taller condominium tower.

The project's developer-owners were intent on incorporating the arts into the guest's experience here—a goal that Bentel & Bentel were ideally suited to meet. Collaborating with art consultants for the owners, they made sure that the integration of artworks went well beyond merely hanging pieces on the walls. Set within surfaces of neutral color, the artworks have become part of the architecture, helping to define spaces and support way-finding.

The hotel's first floor includes a banquet hall, accessed directly from the lobby and looking out into a planted public space created as part of the development. From the lobby and check-in area, a sculptural stair leads to a mezzanine-like second-floor bar and dining area, which overlooks the entry and offers broad outward views. The objective in the public spaces has been to offer guests a continuity of spaces flowing one to another, rather than a sequence of separate volumes.

Corridors on each guestroom floor have been designed to feature one of the seven arts represented in the hotel's collection: painting, sculpture, dance, music composition, film, theater, and photography. The bedrooms are also the setting for distinctive artworks, in this case photographs selected through a local contest. Each room displays an enlarged photo above the long, horizontal, custom-designed headboard, complemented by expertly configured lighting.

The typical guest room is entered through a "peninsula" corridor reaching deep into the bedroom bay, beyond the bathroom. From a hard-floored vestibule inside the door, one passes through a kind of proscenium to the main space. All of the room's furnishings, largely built-in, were designed by Bentel & Bentel.

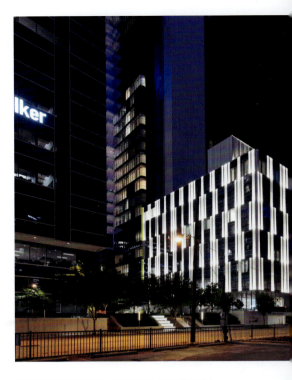

TOP (LEFT TO RIGHT): Hotel in Arts District setting; Entry lobby with *Resistance Reverb: Movements 1* by Lava Thomas suspended above it, *Volvere* by Alison Watt on wall
RIGHT: Stair to mezzanine, *Then I Wished That I Could Come Back as a Flower* by Nekisha Durrett on lobby wall
FOLLOWING PAGES: Lobby lounge and stair

WHAT WE DO HALL ARTS HOTEL

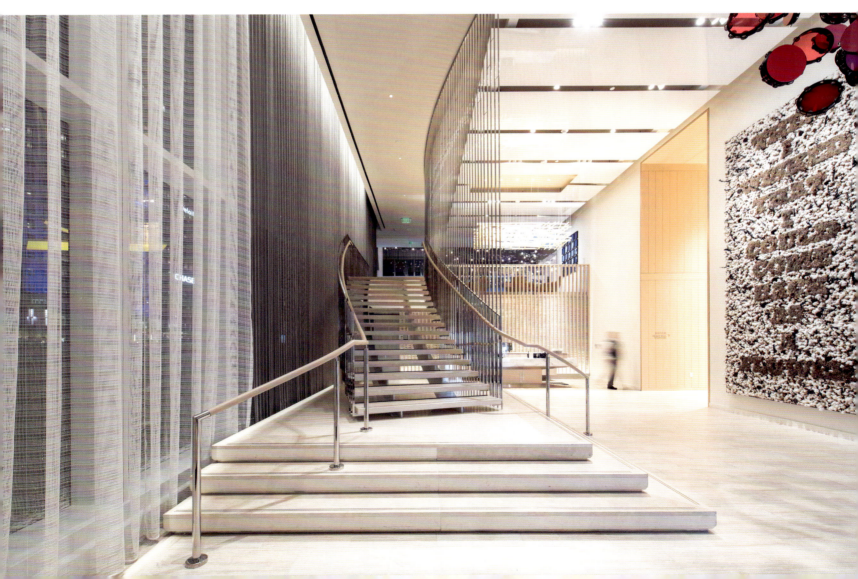

WHAT WE DO HALL ARTS HOTEL

OPPOSITE (TOP TO BOTTOM): Dining and bar with Spencer Finch's *Asteroid* ceiling installation; Conference room with *All That Is Real Is Possible* by Alicia Eggert on corridor wall
RIGHT: Ballroom ceiling light designed by architects with Linda Sormova Melichova of Lasvit

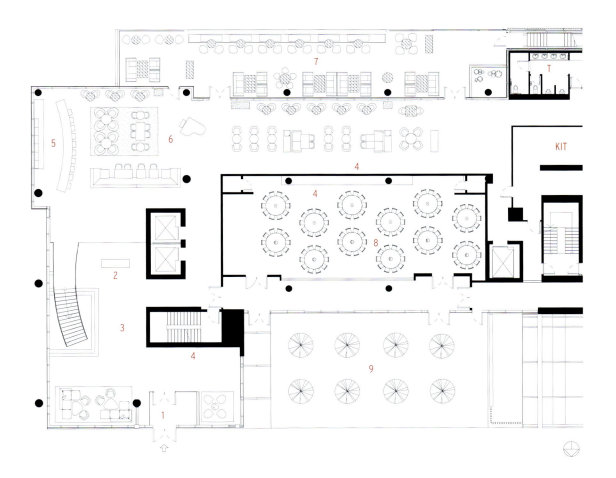

1	VESTIBULE
2	ENTRY DESK
3	LOBBY
4	ART WALL
5	BAR
6	LOUNGE
7	OUTDOOR DINING
8	BALLROOM
9	URBAN GARDEN
T	TOILETS
KIT	KITCHEN

189

CORRELATIONS: LIFE + WORK   BENTEL & BENTEL ARCHITECTS

ABOVE (TOP TO BOTTOM): Guest bedroom; Bathtub with bedroom view
RIGHT: Junior suite bedroom, art over beds selected through a local contest

WHAT WE DO   HALL ARTS HOTEL

CORRELATIONS: LIFE + WORK BENTEL & BENTEL ARCHITECTS

ABOVE: Restaurant front from concourse
OPPOSITE: Dining room with custom lights

HUDSON YARDS GRILL

New York, New York | 2019

At a prime location in Manhattan's colossal Hudson Yards office-retail-residential-entertainment development, Hudson Yards Grill offers a lively, moderate-priced option in a complex that includes several top-of-the-line restaurants. Its design represents New York's legendary vibrancy with striking forms, vivid colors, and a generous selection of Modern art.

The grill's front, on a retail concourse, promises a respite from the futuristic sleekness of the development as a whole. A screen of dark-stained wood louvers, with bright colors filtering through, previews the interior experience. A wide opening, canted at an angle, invites entry.

Seating almost 250 diners in cozy booths and at robust wood tables, the space inside features a rectangular island bar, a highly visible open kitchen, and an intricate wood trellis above the dining area. Acknowledging that many patrons will arrive at busy times without reservations, there is an ample waiting area just inside the entrance, centered on a colorful abstract sculpture by David Hayes, with generous, red-upholstered seating.

The restaurant's lighting plays a major role in creating a sense of intimacy, directing pools of light onto table tops that are, for the most part, fixed in position. The contrast of that lighting with black-painted ceilings, black granite floors, and dark walnut walls provides a feeling of privacy and individuality at each table. Other lighting is focused on the artworks, intentionally with theatrical effect.

The professionally curated art displayed includes works by such acclaimed masters as Sol Lewitt and Damon Hyldreth. Primarily abstract and boldly colored, this collection reinforces a sense of place. And since there are hardly any openings at the restaurant's boundaries, they take on the role of windows into a wider world. Specifically connecting the restaurant to the city and the Hudson Yards neighborhood is a vibrant mural of the Hudson River by Carole Bolsey in the bar area.

CORRELATIONS: LIFE + WORK　　BENTEL & BENTEL ARCHITECTS

WHAT WE DO   HUDSON YARDS GRILL

TOP (LEFT TO RIGHT): Entry; Bar area with mural of Hudson River by Carole Bolsey; Dining area with prints by Paul Bentel
BELOW LEFT: Central dining, under canopy, with Damon Hyldreth sculptures

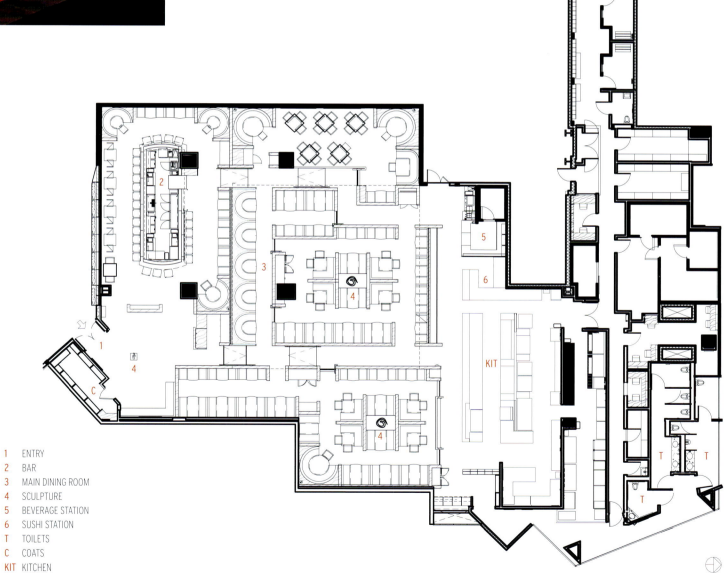

1 ENTRY
2 BAR
3 MAIN DINING ROOM
4 SCULPTURE
5 BEVERAGE STATION
6 SUSHI STATION
T TOILETS
C COATS
KIT KITCHEN

195

WHAT WE DO   SMALL BATCH

OPPOSITE: Dining area under trellis with open kitchen beyond
ABOVE (LEFT TO RIGHT): Entry; Bar and lounge

SMALL BATCH

Garden City, New York | 2018

For this restaurant, chef-owner Tom Colicchio set himself the culinary goal of celebrating, without sentimentality or nostalgia, the world-class products of the farms, fisheries, and vineyards of Long Island. To support this goal the architects' design took its cues from the character of buildings and spaces where these products originate—the barns, sheds, pens, haylofts, and docks of the region. Just as Colicchio intended in his cooking, their design interpreted these artifacts in modern terms—on the exterior and interior—to establish a dining environment that aligned with the contemporary spirit of his food and service.

The restaurant's location on an outer corner of an upscale retail mall allowed Bentel & Bentel to give it a clear identity, disengaged from the more predictable development around it. The crisp white board-and-batten siding of its long exterior walls contrasts with the taller black clapboarded "shed" of its corner entrance pavilion. The exceptional simplicity of its forms and colors sets Small Batch apart from nearby restaurants, while telegraphing the unpretentiousness of the dining experience inside.

The 8,000-square-foot interior consists of three principal spaces: bar dining, main dining, and open kitchen. All three are visually and materially connected yet rendered distinct by the scales and accoutrements of their separate functions. Above both dining areas, a network of white beams and open rafters recalls the inside of farm structures. A black-stained oak bar and the backbar behind it, with window-like openings, both separate and link the two spaces. All patrons can enjoy deep views into the kitchen, with its wood-fired grill and the bustle of its cooks and waitstaff. Simply detailed custom furniture recalls, without copying, farmhouse precedents. Brightly painted barn lights, suspended in double rows over the main dining area and in a single row over the bar, provide a warm glow with a spirit of whimsy.

CORRELATIONS: LIFE + WORK BENTEL & BENTEL ARCHITECTS

WHAT WE DO SMALL BATCH

CORRELATIONS: LIFE + WORK   BENTEL & BENTEL ARCHITECTS

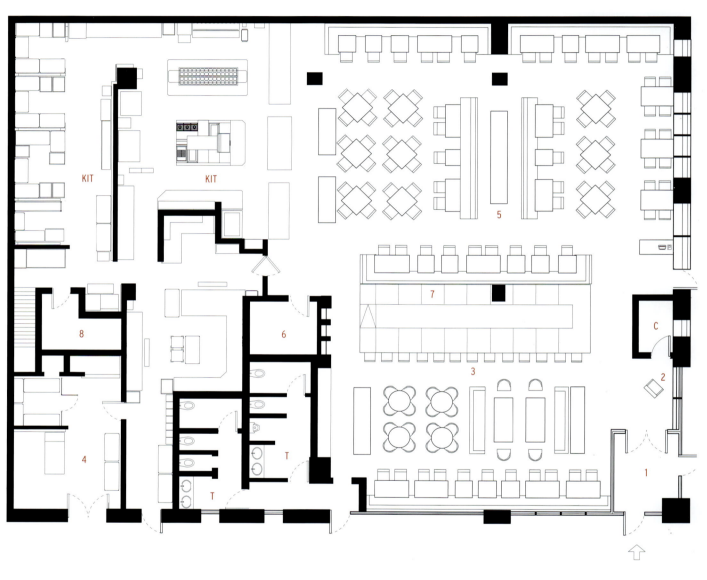

1 VESTIBULE
2 GREETER
3 BAR/LOUNGE
4 SERVICE
5 DINING
6 WINE ROOM
7 BACK BAR
8 OFFICE
T TOILETS
C COATS
KIT KITCHEN

WHAT WE DO   SMALL BATCH

PREVIOUS PAGES: Restaurant from parking area
ABOVE (TOP TO BOTTOM): Dining room; Banquette along dining room wall

CORRELATIONS: LIFE + WORK   BENTEL & BENTEL ARCHITECTS

ABOVE (LEFT TO RIGHT): Restaurant from parking area; Bar with mural by James Kennedy
OPPOSITE: Bar under Moroccan lights

HUNTER RESTAURANT

East Norwich, New York | 2019

Located in a suburban Long Island community, the restaurant was designed for the young chef Hunter Wells. It occupies an existing one-story structure that stands out among its commercial neighbors for its pyramidal, copper-clad roof. To accommodate the new restaurant's needs, the spaces of the previous one had to be entirely reorganized.

The redesign included moving the entrance from its former central location on axis with the tall roof to one of the lower flanking volumes, where a glazed entry with a lighted glass canopy communicates the newness awaiting within. Once inside, the guest sees two distinct destination options: the curvilinear bar straight ahead or the expansive dining room to the left. The back-of-house facilities have been re-planned as well, with kitchens on the main floor and basement.

Surface treatments and furnishings have been chosen in part to reflect the Moroccan-inspired menu. Following the Moroccan and French inspiration, an overall palette of predominantly white and cream tones was created, with accents of dull bronze, which both contrast with dark walnut ceilings and an inlaid wood floor. The bar top is of a boldly figured marble in white, light-green, and neutral tones, with a base of white handmade tiles. Above the bar is a twenty-foot-long commissioned painting in related colors by James Kennedy. A modest television screen is mounted at the end of the bar on its own discreet wall panel—and is covered by a curtain when not in use. A reflective lacquered ceiling and varied Moroccan lights add a festive and magical tone.

The dining room is given a strong identity by a walnut trellis that originates as a vertical screen, rises up into the room's pyramidal volume, then continues into a lower-ceilinged area, effectively identifying it with the main space. White porcelain "handkerchief" light fixtures suspended in the tall volume establish a more-intimate scale for diners below.

CORRELATIONS: LIFE + WORK   BENTEL & BENTEL ARCHITECTS

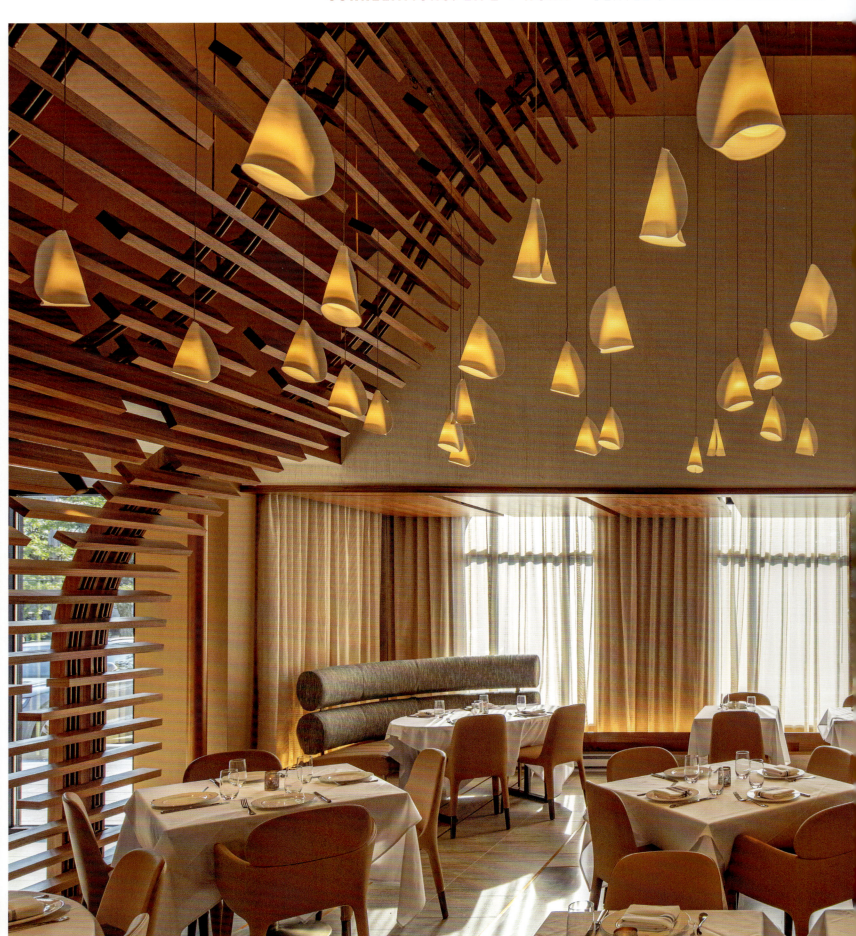

WHAT WE DO HUNTER RESTAURANT

CORRELATIONS: LIFE + WORK   BENTEL & BENTEL ARCHITECTS

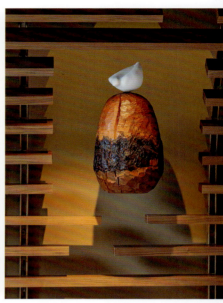

WHAT WE DO   HUNTER RESTAURANT

PREVIOUS PAGES: Main dining room with walnut trellis and lighting canopy
TOP (LEFT TO RIGHT): Terrace with *Spice Towers* sculptures by Michela Bentel; *Egg and Dove* sculpture by Michela Bentel; Kitchen
BELOW LEFT: Main dining room

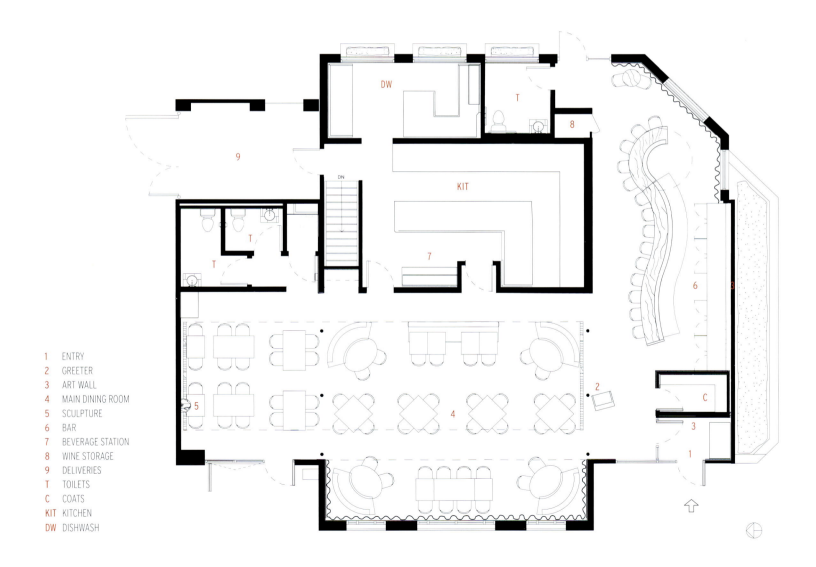

1 ENTRY
2 GREETER
3 ART WALL
4 MAIN DINING ROOM
5 SCULPTURE
6 BAR
7 BEVERAGE STATION
8 WINE STORAGE
9 DELIVERIES
T TOILETS
C COATS
KIT KITCHEN
DW DISHWASH

207

601 LEXINGTON AVENUE ATRIUM

New York, New York | 2021

When the prominent fifty-nine-story office tower originally known as Citicorp was completed in 1977, it was notable for the inventive design of the Privately Owned Public Space (or POPS) it included in response to zoning incentives. The full-city-block Midtown Manhattan complex moved beyond the fair-weather plazas or mere expanded lobbies encouraged by regulations to provide a publicly accessible multistory skylit atrium with public seating, its periphery offering a variety of food venues.

The current owners of 601 Lexington Avenue, Boston Properties, undertook a renovation of this distinctive public space—now named "Hugh" for the building's architect, Hugh Stubbins—to make it a more effective and attractive amenity. Before Bentel & Bentel was commissioned to complete the transformation of this space, it had already been improved with wood ceilings and an area of tiered bench seating.

Critical design contributions to the character of the space include new terrazzo flooring with bold, circular patterns produced by embedding small rectangles of marble in various colors. Furnishings of leather and wood, including custom-designed banquettes, establish a more-comfortable atmosphere than the utilitarian furniture typical of POPS spaces. Ficus trees placed carefully about the space effectively reduce the scale of the sitting spaces, and in some areas establish a kind of arcade over circulation aisles. Lighted glass globes suspended above the trees add a celebratory spirit to the space.

The redesign by the architects includes a stairway linking the main public space at the base of the atrium with the restaurant-lined, through-block, public passage one level above, facilitating movement between the two floors and emphasizing their spatial unity. Adjoining the stair is a mural by illustrator Yuko Shimizu that encourages use of the stair. A second mural titled *Oasis*, created by high school students through the organization Creative Art Works, visually activates the previously sterile passage.

CORRELATIONS: LIFE + WORK   BENTEL & BENTEL ARCHITECTS

WHAT WE DO 601 LEXINGTON AVENUE ATRIUM

PREVIOUS PAGES: Atrium from stadium seating in foreground
TOP (LEFT TO RIGHT): Office tower that houses atrium; Lighting canopy and clock tower with SVA students' 3D artwork in foreground; Dining under ficus trees
BELOW LEFT: New stair with *Water Lilies* by Yuko Shimizu

1 LOWER PLAZA ENTRY
2 FOOD KIOSK
3 OFFICE
4 WINE BAR
5 SPEAKEASY
6 BEER GARDEN
7 SERVICE ELEVATOR
8 MAIN SEATING SPACE
9 STADIUM SEATS
10 ART WALL NO 1 AND NEW STAIR
11 ART WALL NO 2 AND RAMP
12 UPPER SIDEWALK ENTRY
BOH BACK OF HOUSE

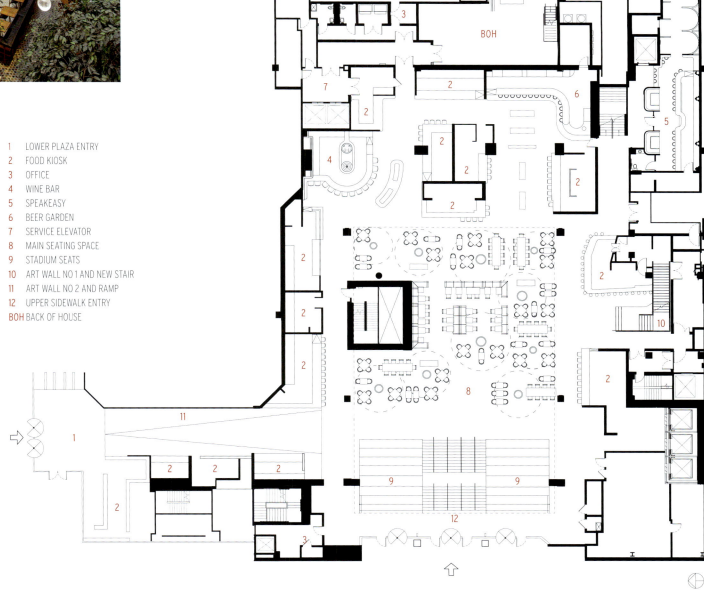

211

OAKLAND PARK DESIGN GUIDELINES

Oak Park, Florida | 2019

Bentel & Bentel was asked to propose design guidelines for public and communal facilities in Oakland Park, Florida, a city of about 45,000 adjacent to Fort Lauderdale. Municipal leaders and residents had come to believe that their community—largely one-story and residential—lacked adequate identity. They were considering whether the design of public and communal facilities could give their city the visible distinction that it lacked.

The guidelines proposal by Bentel & Bentel recommended locating community facilities at street intersections where possible. The city's one-story development pattern would be maintained with structures of pronounced horizontality, punctuated at key points with taller architectural features such as entry pavilions or vaulting over key interiors. Also called for was the conscious masking of the rooftop mechanical equipment and landscaping designed as "an extension of the building space," not to merely add green, but to make exterior spaces. Architecturally integrated porches, trellises, and courtyards were to be encouraged. Prominent gateway constructions for parks and other public open spaces were also recommended.

To support a more positive community identity, the guidelines urged architecture that is colorful, convivial, and youthful in spirit, with a touch of good humor. Design should make buildings "accessible both physically and emotionally." Primary colors—accenting generally neutral-colored exteriors—were to appear with vivid interior hues, enticingly visible from outside. Recommended materials included a wide range of metals, wood, brick, stone, and ceramic tile, while those to be avoided were exposed concrete block, unfinished concrete, stucco, and vinyl siding.

Having drawn up the guidelines, the architects offered prototype designs for a public library and a community center to illustrate the potential impact of their proposal. While the guidelines were not adopted as official policy, they contributed to community recognition of design possibilities for the city to pursue.

WHAT WE DO OAKLAND PARK DESIGN GUIDELINES

213

CORRELATIONS: LIFE + WORK   BENTEL & BENTEL ARCHITECTS

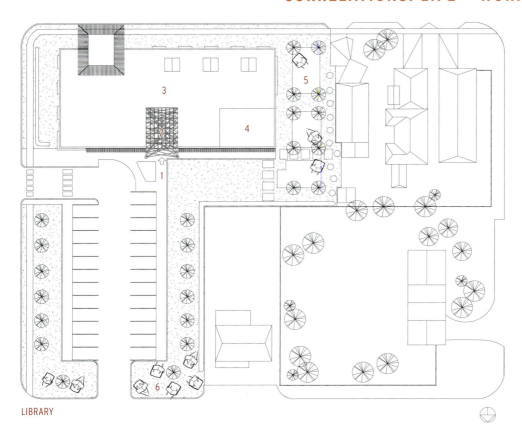

1 ENTRY
2 ENTRY COURT
3 LIBRARY
4 READING COURTYARD
5 READING GARDEN
6 SCULPTURE *THE READERS*

LIBRARY

WHAT WE DO   OAKLAND PARK DESIGN GUIDELINES

1 ENTRY
2 ENTRY COURT
3 COMMUNITY CENTER
4 PLAY FIELD
5 OUTDOOR TREE SCULPTURE

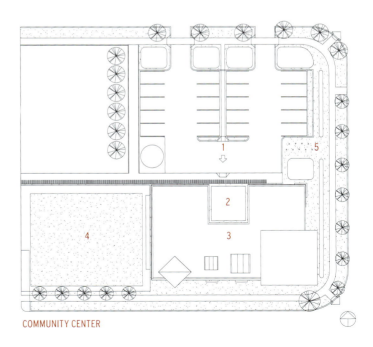

COMMUNITY CENTER

PREVIOUS PAGES: Library
OPPOSITE (TOP TO BOTTOM): Library front; Library rear
ABOVE RIGHT (TOP TO BOTTOM): Community Center;
Sidewalk view of Community Center

215

WHO WE WERE

FIRM AND FAMILY

To understand Bentel & Bentel, the work, and the personalities it has fostered and supported, one must understand the family that lives within it. Unlike most design firms—indeed, unlike most professional practices—Bentel & Bentel is an extension of a family structure and culture. The ambitions of its partners in both practice and life determine the decisions made about almost everything, from the daily grind to the design principles guiding the projects.

To understand the Bentel family, one must understand its origins. A unique moment in history—and a dash of luck—offered the benefits and privileges of the United States to two families that migrated from Europe in the early twentieth century. Opportunities for adults and children alike were available to those who had the physical and mental abilities to pursue them. In particular, the arrival of the families of Maria Azzarone (from Italy) and Frederick Bentel (from Germany) coincided with a period of growing employment in an expanding building construction industry.

The moves to the United States did not mean the loss of family practices. Instead, an alchemy of tradition and modernity emerged. Close family structures remained even while the opportunities of cosmopolitanism pervaded their world. While ambition to experience and garner the fruits of this modern moment was a defining trait for both families, it was always accompanied by family bonds anchored in a dedication to parents, siblings, and extended family. And so, a large number of people coexisted as a support network.

CORRELATIONS: LIFE + WORK   BENTEL & BENTEL ARCHITECTS

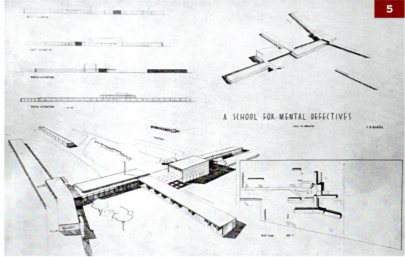

1. Firm founders Maria and Fred Bentel
2. Doris, Gloria, Lucille, Maria Azzarone, Forest Hills, Queens, New York, 1945
3. Charles and Fred Bentel with their mother Maria at the 1939 New York World's Fair
4. Charles and Fred in Jamaica, Queens, while students at Pratt Institute
5. Fred Bentel, "A Project for a School for Mental Defectives" as published in Olindo Grossi, "Architecture at Pratt," Pratt publication ca. 1949
6. Maria as Ramona

WHO WE WERE

Maria Azzarone's Family

Louis (Luigi) Azzarone and Liberata Maria Teresa Massaro were both members of an Italian-speaking community in Westchester County, New York, around 1920. Each had arrived in the United States from southern Italy: Louis from Apulia and Teresa from the province of Benevento. Ship manifests and customs declarations reveal that Teresa and Louis, both in their late teens, arrived without knowledge of English and with little money in their pockets. Teresa's father, Gennaro Massaro, and older brother had come to the United States a few years earlier. Gennaro found work as a mason and worked his way up to mason supervisor on several public works projects in the New York City area, including the Croton Reservoir and the railroad bridge crossing the Hell Gate. Family lore has it that his wife, Rosa Meccariello, arrived with four children, including the eighteen-year-old Teresa, with no warning and hardly any knowledge of where to find Gennaro. Once the family united, they settled in the town of Eastchester, just north of New York City, on a farm shared with other relatives. The farm provided a livelihood for the family, so much so that Teresa learned butchering and business practices there.

Louis arrived in the United States as an untrained laborer and, like Gennaro, found employment in the construction industry. On the basis of his steady work and family aspirations, he courted Teresa. Looking to advance herself as a seamstress, Teresa rejected Louis's frequent offers of marriage. But she finally accepted his proposal—fulfilling a deathbed promise she had made to her mother Rosa—and they married in 1921. Soon thereafter, the couple moved to New York City, where Louis began work as an independent contractor.

It is interesting to observe the forward path of these immigrants. Within just ten years, two penniless teenagers had become a more or less established married couple. Louis had a bank account, a business, and a home as well as a draft card, although he would not become a citizen until 1928. By 1929, he and Teresa had four daughters and lived in a house in Long Island City, Queens, courtesy of a bank for which Louis did contracting work.

Maria Ramona Luisa Azzarone was born on June 15, 1928. She was named for Ramona, the Spanish-American heroine popularized in a song of the era (which earned her the nickname Monie), and Luisa Spagnoli, an Italian business entrepreneur whom her mother admired. Maria and her sisters grew up in New York City, primarily in Queens, moving from house to house when Louis's business presented an opportunity. He set up the Azzarone Construction Company in the 1940s. It was expected that the girls, daughters of a builder father and a mother with business ambitions, would follow careers related to their father's construction practice. The two older daughters worked in their father's firm and eventually married husbands who joined the company. Maria attended Hunter College High School, a selective public school for girls, in Manhattan. Maria continued her education at MIT from 1946 to 1951 as one of thirteen women in a class of 1,145 students, her choice of the architecture course influenced by her familiarity with the construction industry. Lucille, the youngest daughter, attended Tufts University in Medford, Massachusetts.

Frederick Bentel's Family

Karl Bentel met Maria Mueller in the town of Amorbach in Bavaria, Germany, when both were children. Karl was the son of a cabinetmaker—the third son, and hence destined to travel in search of his destiny. Maria was the oldest daughter of the Hofbauer, the principal farming family of the town. Karl and his brother Emil left for New York shortly after World War I, and by 1924 Karl was established enough as a cabinetmaker to invite Maria to join him. Maria and Karl married in 1926 and had two sons, Frederick, born in 1928, and Charles, born in 1930. The family lived initially in the Bronx in a cold-water flat adjacent to Saint Brendan's Church and school, where the boys attended grammar school.

During the Depression and World War II, Karl and Maria were part of a German-speaking community in New York City, living for some years in the area of East Side Manhattan known as Little Germany. Karl continued to work as a cabinetmaker and joined his brother Emil's firm, Universal Bulletin Board, which produced the signs with movable letters that often appeared in churches. When his family moved on to a single-family house in Jamaica, Queens, Karl had room for a basement shop. The boys were never far from the tools and materials of the shop, perhaps an explanation for why they both entered fields involved with making things. The brothers attended Rice High School in northern Manhattan and then Pratt Institute in Brooklyn, where Fred studied architecture and Charles studied electrical engineering.

Fred's work at Pratt seems to have been highly regarded: in his second year, a drawing for a psychiatric institution was shown in a Pratt publication accompanying an article by the dean, Olindo Grossi. And when Fred graduated in 1949, he was awarded the American Institute of Architects medal. In September 1949, Fred enrolled at MIT for graduate studies.

Meeting at MIT

When Maria Azzarone and Fred Bentel met at MIT, they recognized the similarities between their families, both transplanted to the United States after World War I. During their studies there, both were particularly influenced by Lawrence Anderson, head of the Department of Architecture; William Wurster, dean of the School of Architecture and Planning; and Pietro Belluschi, who became dean in 1951. Faculty members Ralph Rapson, Carl Koch, Alvar Aalto, and Buckminster Fuller were also inspiring teachers. In Fuller's experimental studio, Fred developed some of the first prototypes of the geodesic dome; he was licensed by Fuller as a "Dymaxion Designer." Rapson would have a lasting influence on the drawing styles of both Fred and Maria, which were characterized by furniture defined by sharp black-and-white contrasts and an emphasis on the sculptural qualities of space and form.

The programs for Maria's work centered on then-prevailing suburban building types, her later projects taking on a religious orientation. In the fall semester of her final year, she chose as a suburban school project a French Catholic school in Ipswich, Massachusetts, and was commended for relating "modern school planning to educational evolution in a religious framework." For her thesis project she carried the religious theme further, designing a Cistercian monastery that married a spare architectural vocabulary to an austere religious order known for a commitment to manual labor and an association with a severe but beautiful Medieval architecture. The drawings recalled those of Rapson and other American modernists who used strong pencil lines in two- and three-point perspectives to create dramatic images of architectural forms and spaces. Although both Fred and Maria were practicing Catholics throughout their lives, it was perhaps Maria whose religious commitments would encourage the couple to seek out—and sensitively execute—religious work throughout their careers.

During her schooling, Maria worked for Voorhees, Walker, Smith & Smith. Partner Ralph Walker was an MIT alumnus and designer of one of the most prominent midcentury buildings on the Cambridge campus, the Hayden Library (1946–51). Maria recalled that Walker was supportive of her as a woman and an MIT student and showed interest, as an architect of religious buildings, in her thesis project.

Early Work in New York City

Fred would receive his Master of Architecture degree in September of 1950, and Maria would graduate with a Bachelor of Architecture degree in the spring of 1951. After graduation Fred applied to Skidmore, Owings & Merrill in New York, then on the brink of international renown. He asked Lawrence Anderson to contact Gordon Bunshaft, MIT graduate and rising partner there, on his behalf. But at that time the draft was inevitable, and in 1951 Fred began military service with the Army Signal Corps, where he worked on visual teaching aids, including films, at Fort Monmouth in northern New Jersey.

Fred and Maria married in 1952, shortly before his discharge from the military. Maria, who had visited relatives in Europe after the war, applied for a Fulbright Scholarship to Italy and coaxed Fred to apply for one in a German-speaking country. They were both successful. In 1952 and 1953, the two young architects attended graduate programs, Fred at the Technische Hochschule in Graz, Austria, and Maria at the Accademia delle Belle Arti in Venice. Among the other American Fulbright Fellows she met was graphic designer Milton Glaser. In addition to their studies, the couple traveled extensively, visiting major cities in Italy, Germany, Austria, France, and Scandinavia.

After returning from Europe, the Bentels set up home in Astoria, Queens, where Maria's family lived, and they both worked for architects Steinhardt & Thomson in Manhattan. The firm's projects encompassed residential, industrial, and hospitality designs, including the highly visible Motel on the Mountain in Rockland County, New York. During this time, Fred developed his drawing technique, creating quick perspective sketches that conveyed the spirit of a project.

Early Work, 1953–1960

While at Steinhart & Thompson, the couple provided design support for the industrial and commercial buildings being erected by Maria's father's Azzarone Construction Company, as well as for projects initiated by various relatives. The Azzarone company built the Bock and

WHO WE WERE

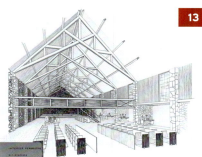
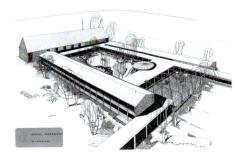

7   Maria Azzarone as a student at MIT
8   Maria and Lucille Azzarone with friends on MIT campus
9   Fred shortly before entering MIT
10 Fred Bentel certification from Buckminster Fuller as a "Dymaxion Designer"
11 Bentel's MIT teacher's inspiring drawing style (Ralph Rapson)
12 Fred, drawing of an efficiency unit
13 Maria's MIT thesis project, 1951
14 Fred with model for a tower during his service in the Army Signal Corps
15 "Wish You Were Here," cartoon drawn and signed by colleagues of Maria and Fred at their departure for Europe
16 Fred and Maria at Versailles during their Fulbright Scholarship travels in Europe
17 Maria at Steinhardt & Thomson office

CORRELATIONS: LIFE + WORK BENTEL & BENTEL ARCHITECTS

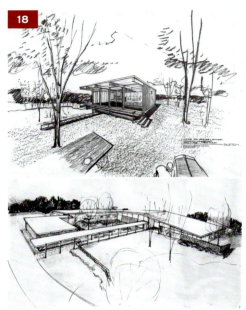

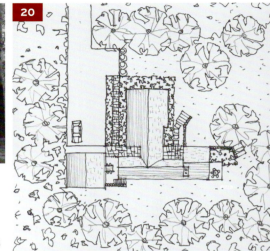

18 Renderings by Fred while at Steinhardt & Thomson
19 Bock residence, East Norwich, New York, exterior, 1953
20 Bouknight residence site plan, East Norwich, New York, 1953
21 Unitarian Church addition, Flushing, New York, 1953
22 Glass block wall from Linden House, 1959
23 First iteration of Bentel/Azzarone House on initial site, ca. 1956

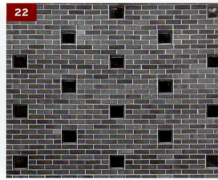

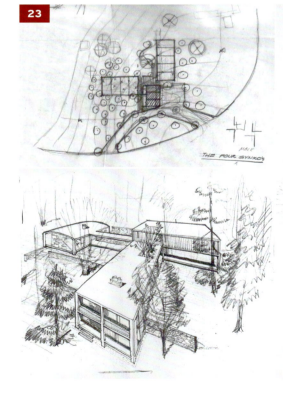
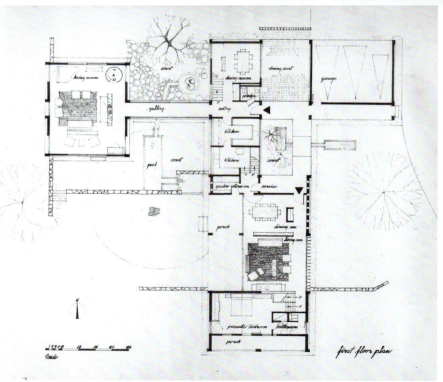

222

WHO WE WERE

Bouknight houses for the families of Maria's two older sisters, which were constructed of cast-in-place concrete and clad with natural redwood siding, brick, and bluestone. These residences show the influence of the West Coast design championed by the partners' MIT teachers William Wurster and Pietro Belluschi as well as the Scandinavian architecture they saw while in Europe. These houses also reveal the couple's response to topography. Both have two-story pinwheel configurations, and both feature distinctive outdoor spaces: an open porch below the upper bedroom wing of the Bock house and outdoor dining areas between the main house and garage at the Bouknight house. The two buildings were technologically up-to-the-minute, with radiant heating and other innovations throughout. The Bouknights had to chain off their driveway to discourage onlookers who were curious about their new Modern house.

Also completed in 1953 was an addition to the First Unitarian Church in Flushing, Queens. The addition, with its spare contemporary design rather than a more characteristic traditional idiom, recalls Maria's thesis project. The flat roof and strong, horizontal lines play against the verticality of the existing structure's pointed arches and exposed wood tracery. A punctuated screen—of glass block in a masonry wall—is a feature they would return to on many occasions.

Fred and Maria's strong design convictions, founded on their family backgrounds as well as their MIT and Fulbright experiences, are demonstrated most strongly in the two houses they designed for themselves and Maria's parents between 1956 and 1959: the Bentel (or Linden) House and the Azzarone (or Orchard) House. These two houses were among the first executed projects of the firm Bentel & Bentel Architects, founded in 1957.

With the design and construction of these houses, the Bentels' careers and family became firmly linked to the development of suburban Long Island. Portions of the island closest to New York City were then in transition from a largely agricultural region to denser development, thanks to the end of World War II, the recently completed highways, and the home-mortgage benefits of the GI Bill. The great estates that had been built for the Pratts, Morgans, and other business and banking leaders were closing down due to the lingering effects of the Depression, real estate taxes, and the opportunity to sell the properties for suburban subdivisions.

On one of their frequent trips to the area in their open-top MGB, Maria and Fred found a parcel of land in the village of Lattingtown, on the north shore of Long Island near the Locust Valley stop on the commuter railroad. It was about thirty minutes from their Queens apartment and only about fifteen minutes from Maria's sisters' new houses. The property, part of the former Meudon estate, had been landscaped by the Olmsted Brothers and was largely flat and well treed. It was being sold by a developer on behalf of the Guthrie family; the land, site of a former agricultural village, had belonged to the family since the early 1900s.

Locust Valley had become something of an artist destination, attracting such luminaries as the painter Fernand Leger and the architects Le Corbusier and Jose Luis Sert, thanks to Marion Willard, beneficiary of the Guthrie estate. An art gallery owner, Willard had established a network of young artists, many of whom were forced to leave Europe prior to World War II, and she had founded a diaspora artist community on her family's estate.

The scion of a wealthy Spanish family, Sert was an exile from Franco's regime in Spain. He had purchased several lots from the Guthrie estate, including the one that Fred and Maria found interesting. Sert appeared delighted that young, MIT-educated architects were to be his neighbors. Even so, the sales contract he drew up included the requirements that the house they built would preserve significant trees, would be "Modern," and would be subject to his design review. So, the young couple, both twenty-eight, were able to acquire a piece of property landscaped by the Olmsted firm, with Jose Luis Sert as a neighbor and the critic assessing the design for their house.

The initial program called for a two-family house with shared kitchen and dining areas for the Azzarone and Bentel families. Fred and Maria developed a sophisticated concept consisting of pavilions set among the trees and raised above the ground in the manner of a Japanese house, forming perches from which to view the landscape. The pavilions would serve distinct components of the program: a central pavilion for a shared kitchen, dining, living room, and workspace; and two separate pavilions, one serving as private quarters for Fred and Maria and their son Paul, born in 1957, and the other accommodating Louis and Teresa. A central bridge or corridor, with one end serving as the point of entry from the drive, linked the pavilions.

Though the design would undergo many changes, the basic concept of pavilions in the woods never changed. Gradually, the spaces between the pavilions acquired their own identity in connection with major landscape elements.

The site topography also made possible separate on-grade access to a lower floor, which was planned to contain Fred and Maria's office among other functions.

The materials the couple selected for the building reflected their architecture training but also their life stories. They settled on a concrete-frame structure with infill of wood, metal, brick, and glass. The concrete construction would include flat slabs but also vaulting, which required complex formwork and non-standard glass infill panels. Meeting these needs would draw on the talents within both of their families. Maria's father, the concrete contractor and mason, built the concrete frame and brick infill. Fred's father, the cabinetmaker, made the formwork and wood frames that carried the glass.

The shared house was to be a true Modern residence: essential forms differentiated by program and executed in a simple material palette deployed to meet different needs in different locations. Varying the infill of opaque and transparent materials provided different degrees of light and privacy in the various areas of the house. The elegant solution spoke to the Modernist desire for a systematic architecture vocabulary based on materials and building methods rather than on historical styles.

During the design process, Maria's parents were able to purchase an adjacent portion of the estate for a house of their own. The architects rethought and re-expressed the potentials of this Modern design method, and the result demonstrates the dynamic exchange made possible by their relationship as life partners and architecture partners. The Azzarone's property had contained the estate's apple orchard. While the land was more open than the property now reserved for Fred and Maria's house, there was a significant grade change between street and the orchard level. Another distinctive feature of the site was a granite wall, seven feet tall, that enclosed the orchard.

The design solutions for the two single-family houses were very different from those for the two-family house they first designed, though they were to be of the same materials and share a similar aesthetic. While the Linden (Bentel) House is a grouping of pavilions distributed through and integrated into the landscape, the Orchard (Azzarone) House is a singular volume perched above the landscape. Whereas the Linden House interweaves outdoor and indoor spaces, the Orchard House plants its feet on the ground, firmly establishing its perimeter and declaring its autonomy within its context.

The Orchard House took on an upside-down organization to turn the elevation change into an advantage. A forty-foot entry bridge led into the upper level, where the major public spaces and master bedroom were located. This positioning created the opportunity to overlook the orchard and also to maintain the living spaces for the older couple on a single accessible level. Maria once wrote that her parents would "have the enjoyment of the garden from its most exciting vantage point amidst the tops of the trees" and that "in the summer, one could pick apples off the trees from the living room." To further connect with the orchard site, "the three vaulted roofs gently arched to assume the outline of the top shaping of the lines of apple trees."

For their own house, Maria and Fred rethought the plan. The pavilion-like structure was retained, as was weaving the building volumes among the trees. But the strict separation of sleeping areas, necessitated by the two-family program, was no longer necessary.

Once ensconced in their new house, Fred and Maria moved their practice to Locust Valley and, for the most part, pursued work on Long Island and in New York City. For the family, the 1960s began with the birth of Maria and Fred's second child, Peter, and continued with daughter Elisabeth. The two young sons spent much of their early years in the care of Fred's parents and their uncle, Charles, working with handmade building blocks and engineering games.

Variations on Modernist Themes, 1960–1970

In the early 1960s, Bentel & Bentel Architects took on the renovation of Stephen and Audrey Currier's Manhattan apartment. The Curriers traveled widely and were design-minded, and the renovation initiated a decade-long collaboration on residential and larger-scale planning projects, which provided vital support for the firm: two penthouse apartments, a family complex at Snedens Landing on the Hudson River, and Kinloch, a 1600-acre farm with its own quarry and lumber mill, in Virginia, near Washington. This series of projects was traditional in design vocabulary but demonstrated a Modernist instinct for simple details that expressed a love of craft.

The Curriers envisioned Kinloch as a self-sustaining property that would support a lifestyle encompassing both indoor and outdoor activity. Kinloch's main house, which was built up around a plantation homestead, was extended out into the landscape in all directions. Adjacent

WHO WE WERE

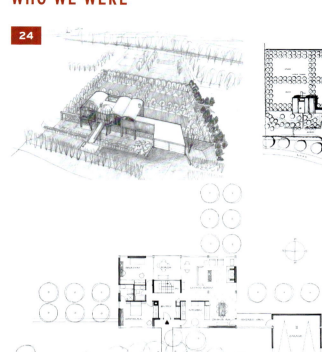

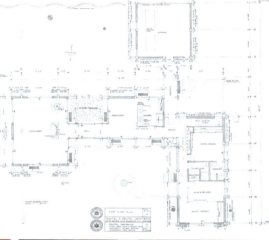

24 Orchard House, 1957–1959
25 Linden House, 1956–1959
26 Karl Bentel with wood formwork for concrete vaults, ca. 1957
27 (Left to right) Karl, Louis, Teresa, Maria, and Fred (facing away), ca. 1957
28 Teresa and Louis Azzarone in front of their residence, the Orchard House
29 Orchard House, 1959
30 Linden House with linden tree, 1959
31 Construction site sign, business card
32 Maria and Fred Bentel, ca. 1959
33 Maria in home office with Paul, 1959
34 Maria, Fred, Peter, and Paul, ca. 1963
35 Paul and Peter with blocks made by Karl Bentel, ca. 1963

CORRELATIONS: LIFE + WORK   BENTEL & BENTEL ARCHITECTS

36 Views of Kinloch, The Plains, Virginia, 1960-66
37 Swimming pool at Kinloch
38 Nivola sculpture to be placed in pool at Kinloch
39 Alina Corporation, Plainview, New York, 1963
40 Medical Building, Elmira, New York, ca. 1955
41 North Shore Unitarian Church School, Plandome, New York, 1963
42 St. Jude's Within the Walls, Napanoch, New York, 1963
43 Maria, Lawrence W. Bell, Father Matthew J. Killian, and Fred with plans of St. Jude's Within the Walls

to its exterior rooms, the Bentels placed open pavilions providing easy access to the out-of-doors in mild weather and carefully composed views in fall and winter. Porches, arcades, and courtyards abounded, each with distinctive detailing in wood, metal, brick, stone, and stucco. In 1961, Fred described their design to Isamu Noguchi, whom they had met two years earlier, in hopes that he would consider doing a sculpture for the pool. Fred wrote, "...we have tried to achieve both indoors and outdoors a series of experiences rather than a single overwhelming statement." The architects took as their model the Alhambra, a complex they had visited on their Fulbright travels, with its intimately scaled and interconnected interior and exterior spaces. These built volumes were experienced in concert with landscaping that included sculpture and extensive water features, which terminated at an oval swimming pool with a Costantino Nivola sculpture that one could swim through or sunbathe on top of.

The Bentels' work at Kinloch also included worker housing, cow barns, horse stables, and greenhouses. It involved historic preservation and adaptive reuse, as well as new construction. And they collaborated with the distinguished landscape architect Dan Kiley on designs for streams, a 35-acre lake, and related bridges. Although working within a complex with deep architectural traditions was at times frustrating to the young Modernists trained to advance a new order of living, it was well suited to students of such architects as Alvar Aalto, Lawrence Anderson, and Pietro Belluschi, who were as concerned with the quality of materials and details as with Modernist forms.

Audrey and Stephen's aspirations to advance a progressive political agenda at a national level were as important in initiating the Kinloch project as the desire for a country retreat. The Curriers' philanthropy, the Taconic Foundation, was founded in 1958 to support equal opportunity for young and disenfranchised communities, and the couple envisioned Kinloch as accommodating a parlor group of Washington politicians engaged in the national conversation on civil rights. Stephen Currier had taken an interest in urban redevelopment and with his wife had supported the non-profit organizations Urban America Incorporated, the Potomac Institute (for which Bentel & Bentel designed the Washington offices), and the Council for United Civil Rights Leadership. His interests in architecture were demonstrated in 1965 by Urban America's support of the revived *Architectural Forum* magazine, which committed itself to addressing urban social and planning issues.

Audrey and Stephen found kindred spirits in Maria and Fred. Politically progressive, talented, and well-traveled, with ambitions built on technical ability, the two young architects were among those who facilitated the Curriers' high-minded political and cultural vision. The collaboration between the two couples was ended only by the Curriers' untimely deaths in an airplane accident in 1967.

Other projects in the office during the 1960s also fostered a particular sensibility about materials and details. Among them were industrial and office projects designed and built with the Azzarone Construction Company and other family members. One of these was an office and warehouse for Alina Corporation, a Swiss office equipment company, along the burgeoning Long Island Expressway corridor. The structure stands out for its clean lines and deep projections, which carry forward the aesthetic evident in earlier Bentel drawings. They also completed a medical office complex for Dr. Henry Cesari, a relative practicing in Elmira, New York. The project anticipates their later work with its flat roof, rhythmic coordination of window mullions and closed wall sections, and continuous band of monitor windows separating the roof plane from the enclosing walls.

Certain of the office's contemporaneous works addressed community architecture—that is, the design of buildings intended to serve groups with shared commitments. Bentel & Bentel designed several places of worship that show their affinity for religious groups. The first of these was a school complex for the North Shore Unitarian Universalist Society. The program called for a series of classrooms linked internally to an existing chapel/administrative center. Instead of a simple block of classrooms, Fred and Maria developed individual classroom pavilions connected by walkways that recalled the bridges for the Bentel and Azzarone Houses. At certain points, the architects scooped out the earth to create two-story indoor and outdoor areas.

Maria and Fred's chapel at the Eastern Correctional Institution at Napanoch, a prison complex in the Hudson Valley region of New York State, demonstrates the Bentels' debt to MIT dean Pietro Belluschi, who exemplified an innovative approach to the design, program, and structure of religious buildings. St. Jude's Within the Walls was conceived by the prison's cleric, a Catholic priest, as a non-denominational chapel inside the prison yard. The architects conceived a centralized plan for the building with seating that radiated from the altar. This configuration was a purposeful response to the authoritarian nature of the prison and avoided the hierarchy implied by an axial plan.

Much of the funding for the chapel was obtained through a campaign to collect and convert S&H Green Stamps (given out as rewards to retail customers), and it was built in large part by the prisoners themselves. For this reason, Bentel & Bentel used a simple structural system consisting of a limited number of heavy timber members and interstitial framing in light dimensional lumber. The furnishings and altarpieces were designed by the firm and fabricated in the prison workshops.

Other fine religious buildings of the 1960s include the Sea Cliff Methodist Church on Long Island (1968) and St. Catherine's Roman Catholic Church in Blauvelt, New York (1968). For Our Lady of the Valley RC Church in Townsend, Vermont, whose previous building had been destroyed by fire, the architects donated their services. These works show that the Bentels continued to be inspired by the craft and material authenticity emphasized during their studies at MIT.

The influence of their work at Kinloch—simple forms, orientation to natural light, and connection of interior and exterior space—is equally evident. Their dedication to serving religious institutions is reflected in their pro bono work as at Our Lady of the Valley and through construction methods that permitted a community to build for itself as at St. Jude's. They would go on to complete over twenty churches and synagogues—testifying to the admiration of their works among leaders of religious congregations.

Fred and Maria's focus on community architecture would persist. In 1968 the architects participated in a design competition for a moderate-income and senior housing project to be located in Brighton Beach, Brooklyn, an exercise in community development conceived by New York City mayor John Lindsay's administration. Critical to the program was the insistence that the complex relate to its environment—both the social environment of neighbors and buildings and the physical environment of the nearby oceanfront. Over eighty firms participated for the $5,000 first place award, and Philip Johnson served as chairman of the judging committee. The Bentels' entry featured medium-rise towers connected by walkways surrounding courtyards, an arrangement that created a distinctive interaction between inside and outside. The project was awarded an honorable mention.

The architects' residential work of the 1960s showed the influence of their experience at Kinloch. The Curriers had given Maria and Fred an opportunity to work with an extraordinary material palette and accomplished craftspeople, which resonated with the construction and craft involvement of their families. The work in Virginia also offered the chance to develop a design approach that emphasized human scale and the linking of architecture and landscape.

The Neitlich House of 1967 was organized around pavilions on a heavily wooded site, creating distinct living zones similar to those of the Linden House. In the Denning House of 1967 (later expanded as the Gambling House of 1973), horizontally oriented masonry walls are set off against vigorous roof forms. The wood structure recalls the work at Kinloch in its materiality and its rootedness in the landscape. Landscaped terraces, pools, and walkways that connect inside and outside at both residences recall the work at Kinloch.

The Bentels' interpretation of domestic life as both communal and compact was further explored in a vacation retreat they designed for themselves in Upstate New York. Ruby Mountain Camp, on the lakeside site of a former garnet mine, began as a camping experience for a family of five—after daughter Elisabeth had arrived in the mid-1960s. Fred, Maria, and children would visit the property in the summer. Fred used saplings from the campsite to make camp furniture. Sons Paul and Peter recall watching their parents walk around the property, gauging views and judging the terrain. The site they finally selected for the house was on top of a gravel mound. The architects did not want to disturb the calm of the shoreline, so the property was set back from the lakeside but still had good views.

The residence consists of a thirty-foot cube topped by a hipped roof and a large, south-facing light monitor. Bedrooms are stacked tree-house style and have balconies open to the shared spaces below. Construction for the upper levels is held free from the exterior walls so that the building can be heated by a central source. Vertical strip windows on each side of the building can be closed with sliding metal doors when the house is not occupied. The formal and programmatic simplicity of this building, along with its material palette of rough-sawn wood and stone from the adjacent quarry rock pile, recalls the austere simplicity of the Cistercian monastery Maria designed for her thesis project and marks it as a work characteristic of Bentel & Bentel.

WHO WE WERE

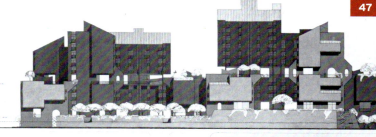

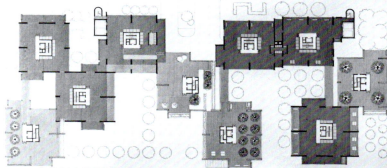

44 Sea Cliff Methodist Church, Sea Cliff, New York, 1968
45 St. Catherine's RC Church, Blauvelt, New York, 1968
46 Our Lady of the Valley RC Church, Townsend, Vermont, 1969
47 Bentel & Bentel entry, Brighton Beach housing competition, 1968
48 Maria and Paul Bentel with NYC Mayor John Lindsay at Brighton Beach housing awards announcement
49 Neitlich House, Oyster Bay Cove, New York, 1967
50 Denning House, Lattingtown Harbor, New York, 1967, expanded 1973 as Gambling House
51 Ruby Mountain Camp, North River, New York, 1969

CORRELATIONS: LIFE + WORK BENTEL & BENTEL ARCHITECTS

52 Hempstead Bank, Garden City, New York, 1971
53 Hillwood Commons, Long Island University, C.W. Post Campus, Brookville, New York, 1973
54 St. Anthony's RC Church, Nanuet, New York, 1971
55 St. John Vianney Church, Flushing, New York, 1973
56 St. Mary Star of the Sea, Far Rockaway, New York, 1977
57 Amityville Public Library, Amityville, New York, 1971
58 Jericho Public Library, Jericho, New York, 1972
59 Commack Public Library, Commack, New York, 1977
60 New City Public Library, New City, New York, 1978
61 Mastic-Moriches-Shirley Public Library, Shirley, New York, 1981

WHO WE WERE

Suburban Modernism and Community Architecture, 1970–1980

By the late 1960s, Bentel & Bentel had established a presence on Long Island and in the northern suburbs of New York City sufficient to gain work of increasing programmatic variety. Their commercial and institutional projects of these years show both the expanding range of commissions available in their suburban environment and their ability to design buildings that were materially rich, humanly scaled, and imaginatively detailed. Applying a unifying vocabulary to varied building programs and within different contexts suggests a design direction with broad applicability.

The commercial buildings designed by Maria and Fred show an expression very different from the flat-roofed structures that then dotted the suburban roadside. Executed predominantly in brick, the Bentel structures often embodied sharp geometries that recalled their religious buildings. A number of such projects completed between 1967 and 1971 demonstrate the transfer of formal and material characteristics between building types and programs.

The Hempstead Bank in Garden City, completed in 1971 on a commercial strip, presents a distinctive profile to the street and a remarkable interior atrium with landscape elements to visitors. Brick cladding gives a consistent texture to the bank's exterior and interior. The building's profile drops toward the road in a series of terraces, creating a low front along the sidewalk. Arched openings penetrate the supporting structure. The combination of tapered building envelope and street arcade presents an urban vocabulary that draws on such precursors as the setbacks specified in the New York City Zoning Ordinance of 1916 and the atrium of Roche Dinkeloo's 1967 Ford Foundation in Manhattan.

One of the firm's most ambitious projects in scale and in intricacy in the relationship of structure to space is Hillwood Commons, the student activities center at Long Island University's C. W. Post campus, completed in 1973. The building complex is situated in a natural depression, a spot intended to provide a future link between the north campus, the former estate of Marjorie Merriweather Post, and the south campus, with its athletic fields and parking areas. The structure combines dining and social areas for the students, galleries, club offices, and performance spaces as well as a large auditorium under a space-frame dome. In response to the varying topography and the need for multiple entry points, a "main street" runs through the building, organizing the program areas in a split-level configuration around this spine; from this thoroughfare, students can look up and down into those areas. The structure of the building further amplifies this experience of interpenetration with a cadence of split-faced concrete block piers, framing both glazed and open interstitial spaces. Crowning this spatial composition are roof terraces that overlook the campus. The firm also produced the graphics and branding for the building.

Bentel & Bentel continued to design religious buildings, but the work in this area was shifting to more elemental geometries, as at Hillwood Commons. In 1971, the firm completed an addition to St. Anthony's Roman Catholic Church and Rectory in Nanuet, New York. The new building features a pyramidal roof form above stone walls (relating to the existing stone church) that weave in and out from under the roof edge. These walls shape outdoor courtyards that recall those of the architects' earliest residential work. A continuous strip of windows separates the roof from the walls. The interior of St. Anthony's is equally elemental, consisting of wood trusses and wood plank roofing, quarry tile floor, and elegantly simple pews.

Two years later Maria and Fred completed St. John Vianney Church in Flushing, Queens. Their design of worship space, multipurpose area, offices, and classrooms carried further the geometric simplicity of other works of the time, suggesting the vigorous forms of Richard Serra's sculpture. The interplay of walls and roof created opportunities to let natural light into the sanctuary in surprising ways. St. Mary Star of the Sea in Far Rockaway, Queens, admits natural light into the sanctuary in a similar way. Here, too, strong horizontal lines contrast with sharply angular roof forms.

The Bentels designed numerous libraries in the 1970s, and the geometrical simplification evident in the churches is apparent in this building type as well. Once again, the topography of the roof creates the opportunity to let natural light into otherwise windowless areas of the interior. At the Amityville Public Library, completed in 1971, ample natural light was dispersed over an expansive interior. As at the C. W. Post Hillwood Commons, the two-level interior of the library offers opportunity for visual connections within a multistory volume.

Amityville was the earliest of a series of geometrically powerful library designs: Jericho in 1972, Commack in 1977, New City in 1978, and Shirley in 1981. In each of these, extended planes with stunning cantilevers highlight the entrances to what are primarily single-story buildings.

This group of structures demonstrates an increasing engagement with the skin of the building: the wrapper is cut to create dynamic interplay between outside and inside and to produce dramatic formal results. At the same time, the ability to construct such configurations remains solidly rooted in the construction technology of masonry-clad, steel-frame buildings.

Maria and Fred would apply a similar design strategy to buildings serving other programs. In 1979 the Urban Renewal Agency of Glen Cove, Long Island, engaged the Bentels to design a multipurpose public services building on a steep site. The strong geometry of the horizontal fascia, like those of the libraries, created the sense of one community building despite the diverse functions within: boys' club, daycare center, and county social services department. The site allowed for individual entrances; the main entry was clearly marked by an angled wall. The Fine Arts Building at the New York Institute of Technology similarly exemplified the architects' boldly sculptural enclosures for complex facilities.

The design language of simple volumes with cantilevered planes that capture outdoor space within the form of the building is also expressed in the Bentel & Bentel office in Locust Valley, Long Island, completed in 1976. In this case, the material palette was dictated by the existing house that they adapted and expanded: wood-frame construction with wood cladding. Nevertheless, the same careful articulation of volumes with extrusions and cantilevered forms is evident, notably in an arcuated form for the studio addition that recalls at larger scale the brackets of the house's porch. Inside, the cuts and slits create opportunities to let in natural light, as does the skylight atop the roof. The entire staff, principals to interns, worked in the central space—on platforms around an open core—implying a lack of strict hierarchy. Indeed, the entire office participated in each project. The year they opened their new office, Fred and Maria were inducted into the American Institute of Architects College of Fellows.

The 1970s were also busy years for the Bentels as a family. Sons Paul and Peter attended Phillips Exeter Academy in New Hampshire, both focusing on the visual arts. One summer Paul built a sculpture studio with his grandfather Karl Bentel on the family's Long Island property. Paul moved on to Harvard, where he majored in the fine arts with a focus on sculpture and printmaking. His thesis artworks, monumental stone arches, were created with sculptor Dimitri Hadzi and architectural historian Eduard Sekler as advisors. Peter spent a gap year at Marlborough College in England, and then studied the visual arts at Princeton. His thesis project, exploring the narrative possibilities of the diptych form in drawing and architecture, was produced with architect Michael Graves and painter Sean Scully as advisors. The brothers spent one summer carving marble in Pietrasanta, Italy, at the recommendation of their sculpture teacher at Exeter. Fred, Maria, and Elisabeth met them after the summer studio and traveled throughout Europe following finely detailed itineraries constructed by Maria.

One of Bentel & Bentel's most ambitious projects of this period, never completed, was the Mitchell Park aquatics structure of 1976. A vast complex of Olympic-size pools for competitive and recreational swimming and diving, Mitchell Park was part of the project for converting the Mitchell Air Force Base into the "central park" of Nassau County. The transformation plan embodied a vision of suburbia more advanced than the prevailing network of roads connecting private homes and privately developed commercial nodes. The Mitchell tract was to be a place where the entire county would have access to open space and community facilities of grand proportion. Borrowing planning strategies from Hillwood Commons, such as the central split-level circulation spine with views up and down into adjacent program areas, the architects envisioned a complex where those passing through could engage all aspects of the program. The Mitchell Park project represents a distinct direction for the Bentels' public and institutional work: a dynamic monumentality, based on their experiments with building technology and sculptural form.

One of their finest buildings of the time, one that indicates the direction their work might have taken had the aquatics center been completed—and had local governments embraced the dynamic Modernism it represented—is the New York College of Osteopathic Medicine on the New York Institute of Technology campus in Old Westbury, New York. This elegant structure, made up of laboratories and lecture rooms, had a programmatic rationale for limiting window exposure. Expanses of uninterrupted masonry wall rising from a grassy forecourt gave the building a gravitas appropriate to this type of facility. On the interior, a three-story skylit atrium provided internal illumination to the shared circulation space. Tightly disciplined and finely detailed, the building fulfilled the promise of Bentel & Bentel's previous work, advancing the dynamic interplay of volumes, light, and shade.

WHO WE WERE

62 Public Services Building, Glen Cove, New York, 1980
63 Fine Arts Building, New York Institute of Technology, Old Westbury, New York, 1979
64 Bentel & Bentel Studio, Locust Valley, New York, 1976
65 Fred and Maria wearing their AIA Fellowship medals, 1976
66 Paul Bentel's sculpture studio, 1978
67 Peter Bentel's senior thesis, 1983
68 Paul on a block of stone, Henraux Quarry, Carrara, Italy, 1979
69 Paul Bentel sculpture displayed at Harvard University's Carpenter Center, 1979
70 Fred and the three children at Parc Güell, Barcelona, 1978
71 Mitchell Park Aquatics Component at Mitchell Field, Hempstead, New York, 1976
72 New York College of Osteopathic Medicine, Old Westbury, New York, 1978

CORRELATIONS: LIFE + WORK BENTEL & BENTEL ARCHITECTS

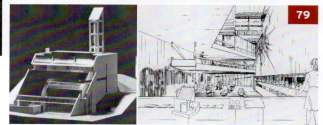

73 Safety and Environmental Protection Center, Brookhaven National Laboratory, Brookhaven, New York, 1980
74 Science Commons, Friend's Academy, Glen Cove, New York, 1980
75 Netherlands Dormitory, Hofstra University, Hempstead, New York, 1982
76 Pegno House, Centre Island, New York, 1982
77 St. Hyacinth RC Church, Glen Cove, New York, 1985
78 Villa Saison, Lattingtown, New York, 1981
79 NYIT/Hempstead Economic Opportunity Commission Headquarters, Hempstead, New York, 1981

WHO WE WERE

In 1980 Maria and Fred designed the 58,550-square-foot Safety and Environmental Protection Center for the Brookhaven National Laboratory in Brookhaven, New York, as the culmination of a conceptual design report on the campus's older buildings. The programs in those inefficient or hazardous buildings would be consolidated in a proposed Safety and Environmental Center. The structure, never realized, was supposed to accommodate three major departments around a spine: police and fire rescue, including a hose tower; administration; and laboratories. The building was designed with energy-efficient features; in particular, solar collectors for power and a Trombe wall for solar space heating. The geometries developed in the earlier library designs, in Hillwood Commons, and in the Glen Cove public services building, were evident in the bold geometries of this project.

A New Formalism, 1980-1990

Had the Aquatics Complex or the Safety and Environmental Protection Center been completed, it would have cemented Bentel & Bentel's identity as an institutional architect for Long Island and perhaps beyond. But the progressive politics that supported such public works waned at the end of the 1970s. The hoped-for suburban renaissance gave way to expanding private development in the form of office buildings and single-family houses in gated communities. The vision of the Bentels was inconsistent with emerging political and economic trends. Fred and Maria continued their work for local institutions such as schools and libraries, but their design vocabulary changed.

A series of buildings, taut modern structures all, for Friends Academy, a K-12 Quaker institution in Glen Cove, Long Island, channeled the school's values into architecture. One of these, the academy's Science Commons of 1980, was precipitated by the firm's master plan for the school, which centralized the music, art, math, and science curricula. But the Bentels' architectural idiom, built on the design vocabulary of their libraries and appropriate to a Quaker school, did not satisfy the emerging, conservative taste evident in both private and public projects. Moreover, the national architectural discourse had shifted away from the values of the Modern Movement and toward those of Postmodernism. While on occasion Postmodernism resulted in an architecture of complexity as espoused by Robert Venturi and Denise Scott Brown, it more often produced a revival of period styles—or merely churned out pastiche incorporating recognizable motifs to mask mundane building volumes.

The Bentel & Bentel practice did not suffer during this period but work that reflected progressive social ideas did not resonate with the same force it once had. The Netherlands Dormitory at Hofstra University reflected a continued aspiration to link building volume to exterior space. But the geometrically clarified versions of historical forms here did not have the vibrancy of the architects' earlier work. In other projects, Maria and Fred experimented with architecture that drew on the traditional precedents celebrated by Postmodernists, as in the Pegno House of 1982. These works and the St. Hyacinth Church of 1985 recall the robust interpretation of traditional closed, pitched-roof architectural forms that the firm developed in their churches of prior decades.

At the same time the Bentels were making forays into Postmodern traditionalism, they continued to advance their dynamic sculptural and spatial work of the 1970s. One representative project is the unrealized Hempstead Economic Opportunity Commission headquarters on the campus of New York Institute of Technology. A similar extension of earlier design principles is the Villa Saison, a group of residential buildings with flat-roofed cubic volumes reminiscent of early Modernist works. Also at that time, perhaps reflecting a renewed interest in early Modernism, the firm's drawing style shifted away from vigorous and romantic perspectives, with deep contrasts of dark and light, toward a spare and unemotional description of form and space. This change was due in part to the use of the then-fashionable axonometric projection, a technique that might be considered impersonal because it lacks a vanishing point.

During the 1980s Paul and Peter Bentel studied architecture at the Graduate School of Design at Harvard. Carol Rusche pursued her graduate education at the College of Design, North Carolina State University after attending Washington University in St. Louis as an undergraduate. She met her husband-to-be Paul in 1982, while she was working at The Architects Collaborative (TAC) in Cambridge, and he was at Harvard. They were married in 1987 at the Church of Santa Maria Gloriosa dei Frari in Venice.

Re-establishing the Progressive Ethic

Starting in the mid-1980s and continuing into the 1990s, partners-to-be Paul, Peter, and Carol began to take part in the firm's evolution. They introduced an energized idealism, renewing Maria and Fred's belief in architecture as a medium of social consequence and intellectual expression. In 1984 Paul and Carol won the Municipal Art Society's competition for the redesign of Manhattan's Times Square, along with seven other first-place entries from a pool of 565 submissions. Their idealism is evident in their vision of a renewed Times Square as an urban theater, exemplifying the function of the surrounding area. The 1985 competition design for the Suffolk County Courthouse on Long Island, developed by Bentel & Bentel in association with Japanese architect Arata Isozaki, involved both generations of firm leadership and demonstrated renewed values and energy. Paul, Peter, and Carol worked in Tokyo with Isozaki and his team developing a scheme responsive to the project's high security demands, at the same time exploring the meaning of suburban monumentality. The younger Bentels were in constant contact with Maria and Fred, exchanging faxes on an hourly basis as the U.S. office developed alternative layouts. Although Isozaki's influence is undeniable, Bentel & Bentel was more invested in the project and more responsible for the form and identity. Ultimately, Mitchell Giurgola & Partners won the competition with a characteristically Modern design solution.

The new dynamism was especially evident in designs for academic and religious institutions emboldened to embrace more dynamic architecture than they would have in the preceding decade. For St. Stephen the First Martyr Church of 1991 in Warwick, New York, the firm designed a building that evoked the character of nearby barns while also expressing the role of its structural framing structure as both vital support and a visual metaphor for the forested site. (See St. Stephen the First Martyr Church, page 63.) That church elevated the firm's standing and inspired trust in the architects for continued experiments with bold structural formalism in projects such as Parish of the Holy Cross of 1995 in Nesconsett, New York. (See Parish of the Holy Cross, page 81.)

Similarly, Bentel & Bentel began to celebrate structure, materials, and natural light organized in the service of a broader community of users. Lynbrook Public Library, an addition to an exquisite, early twentieth-century Beaux-Arts building, embodied a strategy of vigorous "discussion" between architecture of the past and the present while also delivering a light-filled interior enhanced by the building's sculptural framing. Other public libraries would follow, showing a similar engagement between past and present, light and structure. (See Bethpage Public Library, page 72.)

The 1990s were notable for the firm's expansion into the area of hospitality, led by the three younger partners. Works completed include restaurants such as Gramercy Tavern (page 68), Eleven Madison Park (page 84), Craft (page 94), and The Modern (page 98) at the Museum of Modern Art, landmarks that led to more such commissions across the U.S. and abroad.

But nothing was as consequential about the decade ending in 2000 as the death of the firm's principal partner, Maria Azzarone Bentel. Although she succumbed to cancer in the evening of Election Day 2000, she had insisted on voting in person earlier that day. Her determination was no surprise for a woman who focused acutely on getting the job done, expressing an opinion, and establishing a vision for the future of the practice. Maria's death marked the transition between the founding partners and the succeeding partners, who had already adopted the energy and vision shown by Maria and Fred over the course of many decades.

Fred continued to come into the office every day, working on an addition to the family's Ruby Mountain Camp. Always a talented and often amusing delineator, he covered his office and his home (still the residence designed and built with Maria in 1957–59) in pencil and pen sketches. He also continued to teach at the New York Institute of Technology, where he and Maria contributed to the education of more than 3,000 architecture students. He continued to counsel and inspire the next generation of partners until he died on May 30, 2016.

Which leads us back to the beginning, to Who We Are today.

---

80 Winning entry for Times Square Competition, Carol Rusche and Paul Bentel, 1984
81 Competition design for Suffolk County Courthouse, Central Islip, New York, 1985
82 Members of firm with clients for St. Stephen the First Martyr Church, celebrating AIA Long Island award, 1991
83 Lynbrook Public Library, Lynbrook, New York, 1992
84 Maria with students
85 Fred with students and family members Paul, Carol, and Peter Bentel at his final critique at NYIT
86 Two generations of Bentels receiving the NYIT "Friends" Legacy Award, 2022

WHO WE WERE

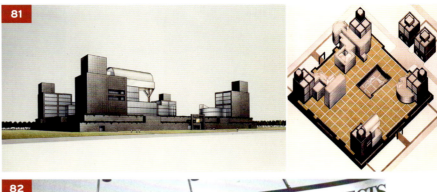

ABOUT THE AUTHORS

Bentel & Bentel Partners

Carol Rusche Bentel, FAIA, trained as a dancer before studying architecture, brings an intuitive ability to choreograph space and movement to the collaboration. As a designer and teacher, her advocacy of conceptual integrity reminds us that design is both a creative and critical enterprise. She has been principally responsible for restaurant, hotel, and institutional design with a focus on art as an essential component. She shares her work as an architect and interior designer with her mission as a passionate educator.

Paul Bentel, FAIA, is a sculptor whose fascination with three-dimensional form originated in his lifelong studies of the human figure in its organic and structural complexity. His focus on skin and structure brings a formal language to the architecture of buildings and interior spaces. In the collaborative environment, his design language is embodied in restaurants, hotels, and institutional projects. Paul has also devoted himself to education with a focus on conservation, historic preservation, and adaptive reuse.

A painter at heart, Peter Bentel, AIA, brings his sensibility to composition as well as allegory, visual narrative, and poetic entanglements of design and program to bear on the firm's work. Deeply engaged in the search for new materials and formal content, Peter finds images of cultural patterns and textures deeply rooted in meanings relevant to our clients, their work, and their communities. Along with the quality of the tactile, Peter's background in theater is evident in the staging and dramatic unfolding of experience present in the firm's work.

Editor and Co-author

John Morris Dixon, FAIA, holder of a professional degree in architecture, is a journalist and critical commentator of architecture and urban design. As editor-in-chief of *Progressive Architecture* for over twenty years he championed progressive and socially conscious design. He has served as chair of the American Institute of Architects national Committee on Design. He continues to write articles and edit books on architecture.

ACKNOWLEDGMENTS

We owe immense gratitude to Maria and Fred Bentel, who provided the foundation that supports everything we are and everything that Bentel & Bentel has become. They taught us not only how to orchestrate the design of buildings but also how to practice architecture with professional and personal commitment. They introduced us to the community of their clients, all of whom understood the value that Maria and Fred uniquely brought to a project as architects and collaborators. They encouraged us to experiment in pursuit of our own architectural and artistic instincts without losing sight of their ethos of intellectual and aesthetic integrity combined with a commitment to the collective enterprise of firm and family.

We devised and wrote this book with John Morris Dixon who was our intellectual compass as we reflected on the history of Bentel & Bentel. As an architectural graduate whose tenure as a journalist overlapped with the period this book covers, John understands the cultural and social context for the work we describe as well as the collaborative instinct that has sustained the first two generations. Andrea Monfried first recognized the collective engagement that distinguishes our work and life. She suggested the title, "Correlations." In that word, she captured a defining characteristic of our work and lives.

We would like to thank all of those with whom Bentel & Bentel has collaborated over the years. Though we may not have been personally involved in the many library, school, residential, and religious projects from the early days of the firm, we were present and, more likely than not, building a model or drafting a detail. We lived through projects such as St. Jude's Within the Walls and the C.W. Post Student Union—as projects in the office and subjects of discussion at the dinner table. Of those early advocates of Maria and Fred, we remember among many others Peter Blake, the Reverend Matthew Killian, Ralph Caso, Audrey and Stephen Currier, Doris and Neil Bouknight, Gloria and George Bock, Myron Roochvarg, and Sister George Aquin O'Connor, and offer a belated thanks for supporting the firm in its early years. More recently, we acknowledge those who have maintained buildings designed by Bentel & Bentel, especially Long Island University, New York Institute of Technology, Webb Institute, St. Anthony's RC Church, Old Westbury Hebrew Congregation, and St. Joseph's University. We owe many thanks to our collaborators from the recent past including the chefs and restaurateurs: Tom Colicchio, Danny Meyer, David Swinghamer, Maguy Le Coze, Eric Ripert, Aldo Sohm, Emmanuel Verstraeten, Barbara Lynch, David Mancini, Ken and Chris Himmel, John Powers, Michael Lamonaco, Gordon Ramsay, Garrett Harker, Paul Grieco, Gillis and George Poll, Will Guidara, Gabriel Kreuther, Pascaline Lepeltier, Jeremy Bearman, and Angela Hartnett; the hoteliers including Kathryn and Craig Hall, Paula and James Crown, Carol Parks, Frank Fertitta, Jr. and Lorenzo Fertitta, Patrick Donnelly, Mark Pardue, and Matt Adams; the educational and religious clients including Sister Elisabeth Hill, John Roth, Donald R. Boomgaarden, Sister Sheila O'Neill, Keith Michel, Burt Roslyn, and Silas, David, and Anthony Rhodes.

We thank the collaborative artists with whom we have worked; in particular, Burghard Müller-Dannhausen, Damien Hirst, Thomas Demand, Per Fronth, Ran Ortner, Jaume Plensa, Robert Kushner, Stephen Hannock, Damon Hyldreth, Petra Cortright, Ben Butler, James Kennedy, and Yuko Shimizu.

We thank our consultants, engineers, contractors, and those who built our millwork, furniture, and light fixtures for their attention to detail.

We thank the photographers who have made our architecture live on in print, particularly Eduard Hueber, who took the majority of our photographs, among other great photographers.

We especially want to thank our dedicated staff without whose vigilance and commitment these projects would not have been realized with the quality they possess.

Most of all we thank our families—including our sister Elisabeth, a fellow rider on this journey, her talented family and our extended family of siblings, cousins, aunts, and uncles—for their support, and on more than one occasion, their collaboration in the creation of our firm. Here's to our children, the next generation—all of them artists in their own right.

Published in Australia in 2024 by
The Images Publishing Group Pty Ltd
ABN 89 059 734 431

Offices

Melbourne
Waterman Business Centre
Suite 64, Level 2 UL40
1341 Dandenong Road
Chadstone, Victoria 3148 Australia
Tel: +61 3 9561 5544

New York
6 West 18th Street 4B
New York, NY 10011
United States
Tel: +1 212 645 1111

Shanghai
6F, Building C, 838 Guangji Road
Hongkou District, Shanghai 200434
China
Tel: +86 021 31260822

books@imagespublishing.com
www.imagespublishing.com

Copyright © Bentel & Bentel Architects 2024
The Images Publishing Group Reference Number: 1544

All photographs are by Eduard Hueber, and all historical and Bentel family photographs © Bentel & Bentel Architects, except the following: Flora Del Debbio: page 20 (top left and top right); Brian Stanton: pages 22-23, 25 (right), 28 (top left), 32 (top left), 56-57 (middle), 58 (top left, bottom middle, and right), 59 (bottom left); Sam Fentress: pages 32-33 (middle), 35 (middle right), 38-39 (middle), 50-51 (top middle), 51 (right), 53 (bottom right), 55 (middle), 76-79; Kyle Koleda: pages 34-35 (middle bottom), 55 (top), 172-75; James Steinkamp Photography: pages 36 (bottom right), 41 (right), 47 (top), 152-59; Peter Vanderwarker: pages 37 (bottom), 42 (top), 52 (top right), 122, 123, 125 (bottom), 126 (top left, middle, and bottom), 128-29; Ben Anders: pages 46-47 (middle); Lasvit: pages 48 (top), 189; Don Riddle: pages 52 (middle), 144 (right), 145; Mark Darley: page 53 (bottom left); Alex Fradkin: pages 53 (top left), 184-88, 190-91; Station Casinos: pages 110-115; Oleg March: pages 125 (top), 126 (top right), 127; Garett Rowland: pages 162-163, 164 (top left and top right); Palms Casino Resort/Alex Acuna: pages 176-183; Lorenzo Bevilaqua: page 237 (bottom right).

All rights reserved. Apart from any fair dealing for the purposes of private study, research, criticism or review as permitted under the Copyright Act, no part of this publication may be reproduced, stored in a retrieval system or transmitted in any form by any means, electronic, mechanical, photocopying, recording or otherwise, without the written permission of the publisher.

 A catalogue record for this book is available from the National Library of Australia

Title: Correlations: Life + Work || Bentel & Bentel Architects / Carol Rusche Bentel, Paul Bentel, Peter Bentel, John Morris Dixon
ISBN: 9781864708585

This title was commissioned in IMAGES' Melbourne office and produced as follows:
Editorial Georgia (Gina) Tsarouhas, Danielle Hampshire, Jeanette Wall,
Art direction/production Nicole Boehringer, *Layout* Thais Ometto

Printed in China by Artron Art Printing (HK) Limited, on 157gsm Chinese OJI matt art paper

IMAGES has included on its website a page for special notices in relation to this and its other publications.
Please visit www.imagespublishing.com

Every effort has been made to trace the original source of copyright material contained in this book.
The publishers would be pleased to hear from copyright holders to rectify any errors or omissions.
The information and illustrations in this publication have been prepared and supplied by Bentel & Bentel Architects.
While all reasonable efforts have been made to ensure accuracy, the publishers do not, under any circumstances,
accept responsibility for errors, omissions and representations express or implied.